The Serbian Revolution 1804-1835

The Serbian Revolution: 1804-1835

Great Wars of the World

.

History Nerds

Published by History Nerds, 2021.

While every precaution has been taken in the preparation of this book, the publisher assumes no responsibility for errors or omissions, or for damages resulting from the use of the information contained herein.

THE SERBIAN REVOLUTION: 1804-1835

First edition. January 30, 2021.

ISBN: 979-8215340226

Written by History Nerds.

Also by History Nerds

Celtic History
Ireland

Great Wars of the World
World War 1
World War 2
The Napoleonic Wars: One Shot at Glory
The Serbian Revolution: 1804-1835
Peace Won by the Saber: The Crimean War, 1853-1856
The Wars of the Roses

Irish Heroes
Grace O'Malley: The Pirate Queen of Ireland
William Butler Yeats: Nobel Prize Winning Poet
Scáthach
Finn McCool

The History of the Vikings

Vikings
Longships on Restless Seas

The Rise and Fall of Empires
Rome: The Rise and Fall

Standalone
The History of the United Kingdom
The History of Ireland
The History of America
Stalin
The Fiery Maelstrom of Freedom
The History of Scotland
Robert the Bruce
William Wallace: Scotland's Great Freedom Fighter
The History of Wales

Table of Contents

Introduction

THE FATE OF SMALL EUROPEAN nations was often dictated by larger global geopolitical events. As the actions of the world's major powers almost without fault swept up small and powerless nations in their wake, ethnicities, sovereignties, and centuries of history were often thoroughly destroyed. Serbia can be in many ways regarded as an iconic example of such a turbulent and tumultuous fate - as the machinations of large Empires decided its fate, destiny, and its independence. But even the smallest of nations can cling fiercely to their identity, to their religion, and above all - to the immortal feeling of hope that is ingrained in every oppressed person.

The Serbian Nation is venerable in every regard, its roots stretching far back in time. Its history was often instrumental in the great scale of European developments, and its position was in many ways the key to its importance. Nevertheless, the fate of Serbia was often directly linked to the fate of the great empires of the world, who coveted its strategic geopolitical position and its wealth of resources. Simply put, Serbia was ever at the crossroads of cultures, at the center of the windswept battlefield of the East and the West, of Islam and Christianity. And it is this position that led to much suffering of its folk.

Serbs emerged as a major facet of a broader Slavic ethno-linguistic cultural group, and were noted in history with the earliest mentions of these peoples. Through their struggle for independence from Byzantine rule, and their shaky adoption of Christianity, this Slavic nation carved out its own place in history through a passionate desire for freedom. Throughout the early and mid Medieval period, it rose as a powerful

European state, culminating with the rise of the immense Serbian Empire in the 14th century. Alas, history is ever-changing, and the Serbian golden era was abruptly stopped in its tracks with the arrival of the Ottoman Turks. Their arrival signified a new era in European history, and a new fight between Europe and Asia, and above all, between two major religions, Islam and Christianity. In the centuries that followed, the Ottoman Empire was a thoroughly foreign object in this part of Europe, and gradually attempted to completely change its identity. The foothold that the Ottomans gained in the Balkans opened the critical *"Eastern Question"* which would prove to be instrumental for the development of the world in which we live today.

Still, even the greatest empires crumble under the eternally turning wheel of history and the passing time. Bolstered by the seeds of hope that were sown in the French Revolution, the Serbian people at long last got a chance to sate their thirst at the fount of freedom. Propelled by the vision of liberty, and ever so chafed by the shackles of oppression, the Serbs rose up in arms against the Ottoman Empire. What ensued is a period of bitter struggle, a tumultuous page in Europe's and Serbia's history that was defined by the First (1804-1813) and Second (1815-1817) Serbian Uprisings. Collectively, they are known as the Serbian Revolution, and were the instrumental events in the downfall of the Ottoman Empire. The following book will attempt to deliver crucial insights into this often overlooked period of European history, and - without a doubt - portray a story of man's inexhaustible desire for freedom and independence.

Prelude & Background

ONE OF THE MOST IMPORTANT factors that needs to be taken into account when the Serbian Uprisings are considered is Serbia's geopolitical position. The Balkan Peninsula as a region was ever the crossroads between empires and religions. In ancient history, it was the boundary between Latin and Greek influences, and in the millennia before, the region was the cradle of some of the world's earliest and most important civilizations and developments. However, with the passing of the centuries, its geopolitical position became even more emphasized. It was a critical junction between Catholic and Orthodox Christianity, between ethnicities and completely different cultural and linguistic groups. Then, when Islam entered the region, the mix became even more volatile and diverse - several religion-based ethnicities developed, destabilizing the entire picture and creating a shaky political background.

The Serbs, a South Slavic ethnicity and one of the largest ethnic groups on the Balkan Peninsula alongside the Bulgarians, the Greeks, and the Croats, suffered a complex and unstable fate after the influx of the Ottomans into the region. Ascending to their zenith in the 14th century, with the rise of Emperor Stefan Dušan the Mighty and the Serbian Empire, they effectively brought the Byzantines to their knees and established themselves as a dominating power in this region of Europe. However, with Stefan Dušan's death and the gradual dissolution of the Empire, made all the more rapid with the sudden arrival of the Ottoman Turks, the Serbian people were faced with one of the hardest eras of their collective history.

By the time of the Serbian Revolution of the early 1800's, the Serbs were a mere subject of the enormous Ottoman Empire for several centuries, without independence and greatly oppressed. Religious and cultural freedom was severely limited and challenged the survival of Serbian national identity - which survived against all odds.

But the flame of the French Revolution of the late 1700's, and the critical changes that befell Europe with the spread of the French Revolutionary Wars and the subsequent Napoleonic Wars, reached the Balkan Peninsula as well - giving rise to the all-important *Eastern Question.* The term Eastern Question appeared in the diplomatic circles of the late 18th and early 19th century, and was used to define the question of the continuation of the Ottoman rule - either total or partial - in the region of the Balkans and the Levant. This "question" was instrumental in the everlasting race of the Major Powers for domination in Europe. By the emergence of the Great War in early 1900's, the Ottoman Empire was known as the *"sick man of Europe"*, and the events which we will discuss in this book were the major contributors to this epithet.

The fate of Serbia was in direct relation to the Eastern Question. Their historic destiny was to be decided in the era of Napoleon, when the world was rapidly shifting - and war was receiving a global aspect. The respected Serbian historian, Stanoje Stanojević (Станоје Станојевић) is famously quoted: *"The history of the Serbian people is almost directly parallel to the history of the Eastern Question."*

However, although instrumental in the unfolding of the Eastern Question, the Serbs were not an independent factor in it. Having to always rely on the support of major allied powers, they stood beside the major protectors of Christian Europe. Initially, this was the Habsburg Monarchy, and to a lesser extent the Republic of Venice. Later on, this role was taken up by Russia - the main rival of Austria. The Russians and the Ottomans were embroiled in a series of major conflicts, known as the Russo-Turkish Wars. By the end of the Russo-Turkish War of

1768-1774 and the following *Treaty of Küçük Kaynarca*, Russia emerged as a major Christian power and overshadowed Austria as the more dominant. Then, in 1791 and after the *Treaty of Sistova* that ended the Austro-Turkish War of 1787-1791, Austria focused its attention towards the west, and Napoleon. This meant that their expansive actions on the Balkans were suspended, and that role was taken over by Russia. The Serbian nation - always seeking the support of major powers in their struggle against the Ottomans - now turned their gaze towards the Russians, with whom they shared a religion, brotherly ties, and the same Slavic identity.

The French Revolution was the needed spark of freedom that would start a raging flame amongst the oppressed Serbs. The rousing of the spirits of the oppressed peoples in the west, and the political disturbances caused by the revolution echoed all the way to the Balkan peninsula - and the Serbs heard that echo. In many ways, the subsequent Serbian Revolution has a similar character for the Balkans and Eastern Europe, as the French Revolution had for Western Europe. It was the needed opening for the resolving of the Eastern Question, and was the very first in a string of conflicts that plagued the aged and weakened Ottoman Empire in the decades before the First World War. Another reason why Serbia played an instrumental role here is its position as a boundary - a "buffer zone" between the Austrians and the Ottomans. The Serbs that lived on the other side of the River Drina, and were a part of the Austrian Empire enjoyed a much greater degree of independence and prosperity. Those Serbs were settled there for generations, having fled from the Ottomans. At that time they were the famed "Grenz Infantry" in Austrian service, border guards that enjoyed a no-tax status and religious freedom, alongside arable land given to them. Their service in exchange though, meant that they stood as protection against Ottoman incursions. This is an important parallel development between Serbs living in two different Empires. Those under Ottoman rule were much more inclined towards an uprising, due to the oppression they experienced.

Now, as we mentioned, the Treaty of Sistova in 1791, and the Treaty of Jassy in 1792 ended the hostilities between Austria and Russia on one side, and the Ottoman Empire on the other. Both sides desired a period of peace, not only to replenish their forces and recuperate, but also to shift their gaze onto the rapidly developing French Revolutionary Wars - and the rise of Napoleon. Moreover, the Ottomans were in dire need of reforms within their own state - especially in regards to the military. Compared to the contemporary European empires and states, the Ottoman were lagging far behind, hampered by the rigorous constraints of their Islamic religion. What's more, a great majority of the Ottoman troubles appeared in the *Pashalik of Belgrade,* also known as the *Sanjak of Smederevo* - i.e. in Serbia. In the years preceding the First Serbian Uprising, a lot of turbulent events were unfolding in this region. During the Austro-Turkish War of 1788-1791, a Serbian rebellion unfolded under the leadership of Korun Anđelković (Корун Анђелковић), and resulted in the formation of a short-lived anti-Ottoman frontier, known as the Kočina Krajina(*Koča's Frontier*/Кочина Крајина). This in turn gave way to the Austrian capture of Belgrade and occupation of the Pashalik of Belgrade for the duration of the war. However, with the Treaty of Sistova, Belgrade was returned to the Ottomans, and the rebel leaders were subsequently executed. At the time, Belgrade (today the capital of Serbia), was the second largest Ottoman town in Europe, with well over 100,000 citizens.

The events that unfolded in these years clearly showcased how dangerous the situation around it is, and that the Ottoman Sultan had to implement some crucial changes.

It was Sultan Selim III that would implement these changes - he came to the throne in 1791, and made honest efforts to reform the Ottoman leadership. He saw the *janissaries* - the elite Ottoman military branch - as the major obstacle to the needed reformation of the army. Their efficiency was coming into question, as did their loyalty. Thus, one of the first directives that the Sultan brought was to forbid the janissaries from returning to the Pashalik of Belgrade - essentially forbidding them to enter it. In 1793 and 1794, the *Porta* - Ottoman Government - introduced two major *firmans* - royal decrees - which brought some major reforms into the Belgrade Pashalik and sought to appease the restlessness of the Serbs that was at an all-time high after the end of Koča's Frontier. These decrees gave a lot of independence to the Serbain leaders, the *knyazes* (sing. *knyaz/knez*). Taxes were to be collected by these leaders, and more freedom of religion and trade was given to the Serbian people. Moreover, this allowed for a bigger emphasis on the development of artisans, well-to-do traders and businessmen amongst the Serbian populace.

And, perhaps most importantly, during this period of somewhat superficial independence, and in the military service of the preceding years, the Serbs could - perhaps unknowingly - practice leading an independent state of their own.

However, the radical decrees of the Sultan caused a lot of strife amongst the Ottomans and gave rise to opposition against the Sultan - predominantly amongst the janissaries. Some of them rebelled, launching a series of attacks on the Serb *knyazes*, which further destabilized the region. These rebel janissaries, fronted by the four *dahije* (renegade officers), murdered the Vizier of Belgrade, Hadji Mustafa Pasha, in 1801, and established their own rule in the Belgrade Pashalik. However, this was a rule of tyranny - the rebel janissaries quickly brought an end to the semi-independence of the Serb leaders, raised taxes immensely, and introduced forced labor. All of this caused widespread unrest amongst the Serbs, who could not endure anymore tyranny. Their leaders sent petitions to the Sultan in hopes of resolving the situation, but the *dahijas* only saw it as a threat to their self-imposed rule. To eliminate the option of the Sultan using the Serb leaders to oust them, the *dahija* leaders stooped to a very heinous act: they hunted down, lured, ambushed, and gathered all prominent Serb leaders, and executed them - some by beheading, some by impalement, and some in other brutal ways - in January of 1804. This event is known as the *Slaughter of the Knyazes (Сеча Кнезова)*, and it caused widespread anger and unrest amongst the Serbian people, who began fleeing into the woods and preparing to fight. The seeds of Revolution were sown.

A Spark to Start a Flame

The Beginning of the First Serbian Uprising

THE SLAUGHTER OF THE Knyazes was certainly the tipping point, and the main event that pushed the Serbian people to commit to an uprising. It was the culmination of a chaotic and lawless period of *dahija* rule, and a clear insight into the fact that they were incapable of efficient and controlled rule. Rather, the four dahijas were somewhat oriented towards criminal behaviour, and the slaughter of Serb prominent figures was a clear scare tactic that went out of hand. Well over 70 influential regional and religious leaders were executed around the Pashalik of Belgrade. Some of the more capable and powerful of these leaders managed to avoid the dreaded fate, either by eluding capture, or by fighting. Many of the best Serbian leaders had plenty of experience in soldiering and leadership - some of it gained in Austrian service, and some gained as part of the *hajduks* - the guerilla outlaws that operated in the mountains and forests, and against the Ottoman rule.

Needless to say, the surviving leaders found themselves in a difficult position. Their prominence could not allow them to hide indefinitely, and all attempts at coexistence were impossible. For a long while the leaders could not agree on the proper course of action, with some suggesting an uprising, while others suggested fleeing across the Drina river and into exile. The two hajduk leaders that were amongst the first to organize themselves and gather disgruntled folk to their side were Stanoje Stamatović (Станоје Стаматовић) known better as Stanoje Glavaš, and Đorđe Petrović (Ђорђе Петровић), known as Karađorđe

(*Black George*; Карађорђе). Well over 500 people quickly gathered around these leaders, yearning for vengeance and freedom from the difficult situation. But much indecisiveness was still amongst them. The first to make a decision was Karađorđe, one of the most prominent leaders amongst the Serbs.

Karađorđe was born to an impoverished Serbian family in the Šumadija region of Central Serbia. As a young man, following his marriage, he came into conflict with either the Turks or the Arnauts (Albanians), which resulted in him killing three of them. Avoiding persecution, Karađorđe Petrović fled and relocated to Srem, beyond the Ottoman reach and outside of the bounds of the Belgrade Pashalik. There, he began military service on the Austrian side, against the Turks, gaining crucial experience as a soldier and as an officer. After the Treaty of Sistova and the end of the hostilities between the Austrians and the Turks, Karađorđe returned to Srem, and briefly rejoined the lines of the *hajduks* as a capable leader. But by 1794, he returns to cattle trading, where he emerged as a wealthy and influential regional leader. Throughout his life he was known as a broody, righteous, rigorous man and a particularly merciless military leader. He was fearless and decisive, and above all a follower of justice. In 1806 he hung his own brother due to rape charges - a clear testament of his iron, stoic disposition. It were those qualities of character - strictness, broodiness, and righteousness - that earned him the nickname *Black George* (Kara-đorđe).

As the heads of influential Serbs began falling in 1804 at the behest of the villainous *dahijas,* Karađorđe managed to keep his own head firmly on his shoulders. At the time, the Turks did not consider him as one of the biggest threats to their rule, and his reputation eluded them. Far more influential regional leaders, such as Aleksa Nenadović (Алекса Ненадовић) and Ilija Birčanin (Илија Бирчанин), were the bigger catch - the dahije rulers feared them for their old and firm connections to Austria, their veterancy, and the influence amongst the people. The group of assassins that came after Karađorđe did not succeed in taking his life: they were repulsed and defeated by him and his men. At once, understanding the gravity of the situation in the Pashalik, Karađorđe promptly embraced the *hajduk* life, eloping into the mountains, eventually reconnecting with Stanoje Glavaš.

It could be freely said that it was at this point that the First Serbian Uprising begins as a distinct chapter in history: the people were shocked and aggravated by the massacre of their leaders, and were willing to arise in arms; the leaders that escaped execution were recuperating and preparing to strike back; and the culminating point was on the horizon. One thing was lacking though: a leader to stand at the head of the uprising. Karađorđe Petrović was the ideal candidate for several reasons. From the earliest moment of turmoil, his attitude was clearly defined: *war with the Turks.* He wanted to fight. Moreover, he was not amongst the influential *knyazes*, nor amongst the wealthiest of men, and was not fueled by personal interests or complex politics - he had a soldiering background with soldier's habits. Alongside his old comrade, the famed *hajduk* leader Stanoje Glavaš, he was amongst the first to openly declare a Serbian uprising against oppression. Formally, he was elected as the sole leader of the uprising on February 15th, 1804, on the day of the *Presentation of the Lord* (Candlemas). On this day, he took the initiative and gathered around 300 eager men and leaders in the small village of Orašac. The main aspect of this assembly was to elect a capable leader to lead the uprising. Glavaš was amongst the first to be proposed. However, he rejected the position, arguing that his experience as a *hajduk* leader was not suited for this sort of warfare, especially in the uncertainty of the outcome. Instead he proposed a more suitable figure: neither a *knyaz* nor a *hajduk*, but a capable merchant, close to the people, but known for his soldier's past and prowess: Karađorđe. The choice was ideal, and he was elected as the leader of the Serbian uprising on this fated day. Action was agreed upon and the revolt rapidly accelerated from that day onward.

One thing that most historians can agree on is the fact that the Serbian uprising began as a sudden movement, almost as a logical turn of events. It was the result of the need of the people to survive. However, the character of the uprising evolved over time, and bolstered by the victories and the advantages, and it became a much more organized, widespread endeavor. One could say that the iconic Orašac Assembly was a needed spark that spread the flame of freedom throughout the region. Nevertheless, there was always one goal that was common from the first to the last day: to defeat the Ottoman rule.

One thing was certain - the four tyrannical *dahijas* in Belgrade had not expected such an outcome. In fact, the complete opposite had unfolded. Their plan to execute Serb leaders had not been fully implemented, and proved to be a bad idea. Instead of instilling fear, the *Slaughter of the Knyazes* awoke anger amongst the people which was the last thing the Ottomans wanted. In hopes to at once remedy the situation before the onset of Spring when the Uprising would certainly erupt even more fiercely - the Ottomans sought to negotiate.

One of the more docile of the four dahijas, called *Aganlija (Aganli)*, was elected for negotiations and headed with 400 men to seek out Karađorđe. He met him - and his men - at a meeting near the village of Drlupa (Дрлупа) on 24th of February 1804. The negotiations did not pan out so well. Aganlija at once made attempts to "buy out" Karađorđe with empty promises, vowing to put an end to tyranny and offering him money and land to abandon his pursuits. Karađorđe rejected the offers of money for himself, but sought an Austrian guarantee for the promise of the ending of tyranny as he could not rely on the Ottoman word. Aganlija denied these requests, and soon after the negotiations ended the first major armed clash of the First Serbian Uprising occured - the **Battle of Drlupa**. Some historians claim that Aganlija didn't actually head out to negotiate, but rather to lure Karađorđe out into open battle. The clash was fierce and left the Ottoman leader wounded in the leg - but the battle itself was inconclusive. However, it was the Ottomans that fled the field and retreated to Belgrade, to many the outcome was seen as a crucial Serbian statement.

As such, this first success was a huge morale boost for the Serbian people, and served to cement Karađorđe's reputation and credibility. In turn, this instigated an even greater influx of fighters and volunteers that bolstered the numbers of the Serbian army. By early March 1804, this provisional army numbered around 10,000 men, with more arriving by the day. The Ottomans in Belgrade however, were in a full-on panic mode. This is perfectly pictured by the extant letter of one of the four *dahija* leaders to his own brother, in which he writes amongst other things that *"the situation is such that the brain cannot fully comprehend it! May Allah turn it all to luck..."* However, Allah had little to do with the events that were unfolding. It was becoming clear to the *dahijas* that their action has caused immense repercussions, and that they placed themselves in a dire situation. In turn as the Serbian rebels were burning Ottoman outposts and nearing Belgrade the *dahijas* sought aid from all sides, and hoped for negotiations.

But to the Serbs, there were some harsh truths to be acknowledged. There was the awareness that independently - they could not hope for a decisive successful outcome. They lacked provisions, ammo, weapons, gunpowder, and general supplies. Foreign support was almost mandatory in the conflict against the Ottomans, even if the price was becoming a protectorate. Austria was the foremost support that they hoped for early on. Karađorđe himself wrote to the Serb commanders in Zemun, in service of the Austrians, seeking aid. In these letters - some written as early as April 1804 he even places the leadership in their hands, all in search of their support. Alas, Austria remained at the side, mostly due to the political picture. To appease the Ottomans, they formally forbade emigration from Serbia, and the sale of weapons and ammunition. But secretly perhaps as a form of support illegal trade in ammo and weapons was largely allowed. Seeking to mediate between the two sides, the Austrians arranged negotiations between the Serbs and the Ottomans - on neutral ground, in the town of Zemun (Земун). This meeting was held on April 28th 1804, but no agreement was reached.

Eventually, the Austrians rejected Serbian proposals it was after all just a rebelled region of a larger Ottoman Empire that was in question, and the Austrian Emperor could not risk to involve itself in a greater conflict as the threat of Napoleon was greater than ever.

The next viable ally that the Serbs turned to was Russia - a brotherly nation in every aspect. Both Serbs and Russians shared a lot in common such as the same Orthodox faith, same Slavic identity, similar languages, and a history intertwined through the ages. What's more, several decades before, Imperial Russia welcomed an influx of Serbian settlers as protectors of Russian borders, who were settled in special administrative regions called Slavo-Serbia (Славено-Сербія, Славеносрбија) existing from 1753 to 1764; and Novoserbia (Новосербія) existing from 1752 to 1764. These settlers gave many prominent commanders to Imperial Russia, many of which (and their descendants) would serve as renowned Russian generals during the Napoleonic Wars. The most prominent of these Serb generals and counts were Georgi Emmanuel, Nikolay Bogdanov, Ivan Shevich, the famed Mikhail Miloradovich, Peter Mikhailovich Kaptzevich, Ilya Duka, Nikolay Depreradovich, Peter Ivelich, and many others. By May 3rd 1804, Serbian leadership were in touch with Russian officials and by June of that same year, a Serbian delegation was received in Petrograd (now Saint Petersburg), but received only monetary support to the amount of 5,000 *ducats* and not much more. However, Russia was willing to provide backing for their cause in the Ottoman capital, and advised the Serbian leadership to stick to their cause and not give up the fight. This further strengthened Serbian morale.

During these failed negotiations, the *dahijas* increasingly bickered amongst themselves, and attempted to stop the uprising by any means, reverting to bribery and lies. As every new negotiation failed, and the Turks repeatedly refused Serbian requests, conflicts did not cease. By March of 1804, the Serbian fighters were making fast progress against the surprised Ottomans. On March 18th they liberated the city of Rudnik, and soon after won two decisive battles at Batočina (Баточина) and Jagodina (Јагодина). On April 4th, Karađorđe liberated the major town of Kragujevac (Крагујевац). The news of Serb victories spread far - one of the major French newspapers of the time, "*Le Moniteur*", reported on the Battle of Batočina on April 12th: "*The other day a fierce and bloody battle was led at Batočina. The rebels surrounded this town which held a garrison of 400 Turks who desperately fought. After several hours of fighting, they were defeated and almost all of them died. A hundred Serbian rebels also died.*"

The French report indicates the gravity of the situation in the Pashalik of Belgrade, and the fact that the Serbian fight for freedom was quickly becoming a thing of great importance in European affairs. The Ottomans began realizing this as well, as by late March the Serbs were now very close to Belgrade. Panic took over in the town, and the *dahijas* desperately sought aid from all sides, particularly from Bosnia and Vidin in today's Bulgaria. But the fact that the Serbs now rose in the major territory south of rivers Sava and Danube, and that they were becoming increasingly organized in their fight, finally attracted the attention of the Ottoman capital, Constantinople otherwise known today as Istanbul.

A Crucial String of Victories

The Developments of 1804

BY MID MARCH 1804, the Serbs managed to achieve a string of small but very significant victories, and soon brought the battle to Šabac, the third most important city in the Pashalik of Belgrade. However, it was here that they would feel the bitter taste of defeat, at the Battle of Čokešina (Бој на Чокешини) - one of the first losses in the First Serbian Uprising.

This battle was fought on April 28th 1804, and became known in history as the *Serbian Thermopylae*. On this day, the Serbian fighters sought to engage the Ottoman army that was travelling from Bosnia in order to relieve the besieged troops in Šabac. However, their indecisiveness and the inability of the leaders to agree on the correct course of action left only a small force under the command of two brothers, Gligorije and Janko Nedić (Браћа Недић). This contingent numbered just 303 fighters, who now faced an approaching Ottoman army that was roughly 2,000 men strong. The decisive engagement occurred near the Monastery of Čokešina, in rough terrain, and saw the two brothers and their men fighting a desperate fight. In the end almost all Serb fighters died, while the Ottomans suffered over a thousand dead. The outcome is considered a Pyrrhic victory for the Turks, and was a big blow to their morale. It is documented that the brothers Nedić - who refused to flee - fought back to back, dying in the same way. They were found on the field of battle after five days, alongside some 300 dead soldiers. The Serbs fought as long as they had ammo, and were then defeated in a mass Ottoman charge and hand to hand combat. The "Serbian Thermopylae", so akin to that ancient Spartan battle, was one of the clear insights into the ferocity of the uprising, and that it was now growing into an engagement of historic importance.

By the Spring of 1805, the situation was becoming even more serious. The Serbs sent a delegation to Russia in search of aid, headed by Prota Mateja Nenadović, one of the major Serb leaders and diplomats. In Russia, they met with Adam Jerzy Czartoryski, the foreign minister of the Russian Empire. However, due to the political situation in Europe at the time, help from Russia could not be given - instead, Czartoryski advised the Serbian delegation to plead their cause directly to Constantinople. This led to the Serbian command to seek aid elsewhere in Christian Europe: some assistance was given to them by Constantine Ypsilantis, the Greek Prince of Moldavia and Wallachia. By this time, the Ottoman Sultan, Selim III, altogether changed his attitude towards the Serbs once he fully realized the gravity of the situation: he now declared them rebels, and sought to quickly reaffirm his control in the Pashalik of Belgrade, where the situation was out of hand.

One of the major insights in just how disorderly and how weakened the Ottoman Empire was becoming, is the fact that there was very little regular Ottoman army in Belgrade. The real power was held by one of the major commanders of the four *dahijas,* a mercenary leader by the name of Halil-Aga Gushanatz. He and his mercenary troops - notorious for being lawless and ruthless - held the actual power in the Pashalik of Belgrade. This caused growing concerns amongst the Ottoman government in Porte. Seeing that the situation with the Serbs was already getting out of control and that the rule in Belgrade needed to be reasserted, the Ottoman government installed a new high official to rule in the capital of the Pashalik - Hafiz-Mustafa Pasha. This prominent man was installed as the leader of all Ottoman troops in the major town of Nish (Ниш) apparently at the suggestion by Napoleon Bonaparte. He was also known for his great hatred of Serbs, as well as his ruthless nature. His title "Hafiz", was given to those who memorised the entire holy book of Quran - which denoted great devotedness to Islam. After taking control of this army, Hafiz Pasha was to march on Belgrade and re-establish control.

However, the Serbian command - which was already bolstered with several key victories in the field - decided that Hafiz Pasha and his army couldn't be allowed reach Belgrade. If they were it would greatly endanger the successes of the Serbs thus far. It was decided that the Serbian revolutionaries were to stop the Ottoman army's passage at all costs.

The result was a set of decisive clashes in August of 1805, of which the most famous one is known as the Battle of Ivankovac (Бој на Иванковцу). It occurred on August 18th, and was a clear insight into the seriousness of the Serbian Uprising. The Ottoman army numbered around 15,000 men - and was on the march from Nish to Belgrade under the command of Hafiz-Mustafa Pasha. The Serbs expected the movement and predicted the route, planning to confront the Ottomans at a strategically advantageous position. The Serbian army numbered roughly 7,000 men - and was divided into two groups. One, under the command of Karađorđe, took up positions on the hills on the left side of the Velika Morava river. The other half took up positions on the opposite side, guarding another major route towards the capital city.

On the hilly terrain, in expectation of the Ottomans, the Serbs took up a favorable position and hastily entrenched themselves. They utilized the common entrenchment methods of the Napoleonic Era: simplified earthwork redoubts and palisades, which would effectively protect the body of a soldier while allowing clear shooting downrange.

The Ottoman commander, Hafiz-Mustafa Pasha suspected and quickly confirmed that the Serbs would be blocking the passage of his army, and quickly attempted to avoid battle. He attempted to bribe one of the Serbian commanders, the famed Milenko Stojković, by promising wealth and riches if he would let them pass. The latter staunchly refused, famously replying that the Ottomans could only pass *over my own head and the heads of my soldiers*. Seeing that he could not pass without giving battle, Hafiz-Mustafa attacked on August 18th.

The initial stages of the Battle of Ivankovac were marked by vicious Ottoman cavalry charges - many of which were repulsed by repeated volleys of fire from the redoubts. The cavalry was soon bolstered by waves of charges by the Ottoman infantry, and they eventually managed to capture one of the redoubts. The fight soon devolved into a ruthless hand to hand conflict - sabres and knives promptly replaced pistols and muskets. After conquering one of the redoubts, the Ottomans concentrated their efforts to the second one and after an hour of fighting, it too had fallen. This left only the largest redoubt under the Serbian command: it was subjected to wave upon wave of Ottoman attacks, all of which were successfully repulsed. Towards the end of the day, the Serbian leader Karađorđe managed to maneuver his troops towards a strategic position that exposed the Ottoman left flank and placed their army in great danger. After continued casualties and this new threat, the Ottomans retreated from the field of battle under the cover of the night. The Ottomans suffered immense casualties: out of 15,000 troops deployed, around 10,000 were left dead on the field of battle. In comparison, the Serbian freedom fighters suffered less than a 1000 dead. In this battle, Hafiz-Mustafa Pasha himself was seriously wounded, and soon after died from his wounds. The Battle of Ivankovac was the first full-scale battle between the Serbs and the Ottoman Empire, up to that point, all the battles were led against the forces of the rebellious *dahija* rulers from Belgrade. As such, this major Serbian victory was an enormous boost to their morale, and echoed through Europe. It showed to the Ottoman government that the situation in Serbia was serious in every regard - and that the Serbs were not going to give up the fight.

The death of Hafiz Pasha and his major defeat came as a shocking surprise for the Ottoman government in Istanbul. The capabilities of the Serbian freedom fighters became clear, as was their daring. This brought new determination amongst the Ottoman command, and they were now adamant in quelling the uprising. By September 1805 they began preparations for a large offensive against the Serbian forces. The newly appointed vizier of Rumelia (Ottoman term for the region of Balkans) was instructed to attack with his forces from the South, while the *vali* (Ottoman governor) of the Bosnia vilayet (province), Seid-Mustafa Pasha, was to direct his force into an attack from the west. The Serbs too were well aware of the situation that was awaiting them: after such a resounding victory they knew that a firm Ottoman response was soon going to follow. That is why they decided to stop any and all giving of taxes, and do direct all their resources towards arming themselves.

In the meantime, the armed movement was spreading like wildfire in many of the areas inhabited by Serbs that were under Ottoman oppression. Moreover, the figure of Karađorđe was becoming increasingly popular amongst the people, undoubtedly emphasized by the string of victories his army achieved. In a time when news travelled slowly, and communication was still lagging far behind the Western Europe, the spread of information was often left in the hands of travelling singers. The Slavic "bards" and "skalds" followed the age old traditions and sang of great battles and lofty deeds with the accompanying "gusle" instrument. In this way, the news of the uprising and of Karađorđe's deeds quickly spread through the Serb lands. In one regard, just the news of the successful uprising were enough to instill a flame in the hearts of many eager and freedom-yearning Serbs causing the freedom movement to grow bigger and more restless. This in earnest overshadowed all and any attempts at official and political calming of the situation. This flame was particularly spreading in the *Herzegovina* region, where the desire to fight was ever high. Even from the 1804 and the early stages of the uprising, the Serbs in the Montenegro region were pressuring their local leaders to march and join their brothers in the Belgrade Pashalik. Around the summer in 1805, one such smaller uprising erupted in Montenegro, but was eventually quelled by the able Ottoman commander, Süleyman Paşa Skopljak. Eighteen Montenegrin Serb leaders were hanged in the Drobnjak region.

In the meantime, there was a noticeable shift in the balance between the European powers. With the rise of Napoleon and the first stages of the Napoleonic wars, things were quickly becoming complicated. Near the end of 1805, Austria and Russia suffered a catastrophic defeat at Austerlitz, fighting against Napoleon. This resulted in the great diminishing of Austrian power, especially in Germany, which was becoming shadowed by the French. This in turn meant that the Austrians were growing desperate not to lose their influence in the Balkan peninsula for fear of losing the backbone of their empire. These shifts in turn emphasized the Serbian position and the question of the uprising. Napoleon was quick to understand its importance and to utilize it for his own gains. As the French victories at Ulm and Austerlitz left Europe in shock, the Ottomans were growing near to Napoleon. Sultan Selim III was now convinced that siding with the anti-French coalition would end in the defeat for the Ottomans, and that placed them once more on the opposite side of the Russians. Napoleon jumped at the chance to increase his popularity in Istanbul, and sought to form an anti-Russian alliance with the Ottoman government. To do this, he placed a big emphasis on the events unfolding in the Balkans. He sent envoys amongst the Serbs in attempts to undermine Russian influence there, and was adamant in reasserting the facts that the Russians were to blame for inciting the armed uprising amongst the Serbs. Napoleon had a full grasp of the situation, and used the so-called "Serbian question" to continuously inflame the already fragile Russo-Turkish relations.

What is more, Napoleon wrote a personal letter to Sultan Selim III on June 20th 1806, in which he stated that the Serbian Uprising was a direct product of the Russian diplomacy. He then advised the Sultan to no longer allow the Russians to participate in any further Serbo-Turkish relations or negotiations. In that same letter, Napoleon ominously advised the Sultan to use the "fiercest measures" against the Serbs.

All the while, the Serbs were continuously adapting to the situation on the ground as most of their pleas to the major powers fell on deaf ears. They continued their military preparations and maintained their victory streaks. 1806 was the year in which the Ottomans were amassing troops for what was to be in their view the final confrontation with the Serbs. The Sublime Porte was planning a three-pronged attack on the Serbian lands: from *Vidin* in modern day Bulgaria, from *Nish* in modern day Serbia, and from Bosnia. Such an attack, with a great number of troops, would leave little options for the Serb rebels. However, the Serbs were manoeuvring in hopes of mounting a successful defence. In early 1806 they liberated the east Serbian cities of Negotin and Poreč; took Paraćin, Razhanj, Aleksinac, and Kruševac, and continued to penetrate further to the Southeast. These operations would hopefully allow them to await the Ottomans in the best positions and to be as prepared as possible. In the Pomoravlje district, between the towns of Aleksinac and Razhanj, a series of field fortifications were erected, and became known as *Deligrad*. All of these operations were the beginning stage of a major stage of the First Serbian Uprising.

By June, the Ottoman offensive was now in full swing. However, the initial stages were not successful. Milenko Stojković managed to stop the roughly 18,000 strong Ottoman army from Vidin on june 24th, near Porech. Serbs also managed to push further South, but were stopped near Novi Pazar.

As August came, one of the major battles of the entire Serbian Revolution occurred - the Battle of Mišar.

The Ottoman armies from the direction of Bosnia were now rapidly advancing across the Machva river and into the major city of Šabac, from which they drove the Serbian garrison and re-conquered the city. This major Ottoman army, numbering roughly 40,000 men, was commanded by several major commanders, the chief of which was Süleyman Paşa Skopljak. From here, the Ottomans could connect with a smaller army from Srebrenica, commanded by Haji-Beg, and continue towards Belgrade with the massive force. However, the Serbs responded accordingly, and Karađorđe was quick to move his troops close to Šabac in order to attempt to cut off the Ottoman approach to Belgrade. However, he realized the sheer numerical advantage of the Turks, and thus knew that a pitched battle would be strategic suicide for the Serbian force. Thus, he once again showcased his ability to adapt to the situation, and exploiting the terrain and the force at his disposal he gained a tactical upper hand. To block the road from Šabac to Belgrade, Karađorđe chose a suitable hill, called Mišar, which he proceeded to thoroughly entrench. Here, his experience from the Austrian army was clearly shown, as well as his understanding of the modern European military practices. The hill position was surrounded by an irregular square system of trenches and palisades. At every corner, Karađorđe placed cannons, of which his force only had a limited number. The soldiers were placed along the main trench lines, which were protected by breastworks and sharpened stakes. The riflemen were placed in two lines, allowing for almost continual fire as one line could fire as the other reloaded its muskets. This fortified position gave the Serbian forces an unobstructed view for 2 kilometers in every direction, which gave a good insight into Turkish movements. However, the Serbs were still devastatingly inferior in numbers: Karađorđe's 9,000 soldiers were facing a massive force of 40,000 Ottoman units with a good amount of cannons and a strong cavalry core. However, Karađorđe did not "place all of his eggs in one basket" - he too commanded a modest cavalry force, which he wisely hid outside of Ottoman view.

The battle began on August 13th in its early stage. The Ottomans were seemingly well aware of their numerical advantage: their command crossed the small river at the foot of the hill, and quickly established battle formations. Following fierce cannon fire by the Ottoman artillery, their cavalry followed in what was to be a singular and devastating attack. However, the Serbian forces predicted such an attack, and the Ottoman horses were soon decimated by a system of crude traps and sharpened stake palisades. The Turkish cavalry suffered immense casualties, mowed down by the repeated volleys of Serbian musket fire. Following this, the Ottoman infantry placed pressure on the fortifications, and the battle was soon turning to their favor. Just as things were seemingly decided in Ottoman favor, Karađorđe played his "ace in the sleeve" - the cavalry units hidden in the nearby forest were given command to join the fray. They swept down on the exposed Ottoman flank and devastated it, causing catastrophic casualties. This proved to be a decisive move and a shrewd strategic gambit by the Serbian commander: the Turks were soon decimated and in an all out retreat. The victory at Mišar was a military marvel: the Ottomans never expected such an outcome, nor did the rest of Europe. Napoleon himself - who sent aid to the Turks in forms of cannons used in this battle - was amazed, and gave recognition to Karađorđe and his victory. Needless to say, the victory served as an immense boost for Serbian morale. The Ottomans suffered catastrophic casualties: close to 6,000 dead - compared to roughly 500 dead soldiers on the Serbian side. Furthermore, the core of Ottoman high command was killed during the battle.

Almost immediately afterwards, the Serbs managed to capitalize on this victory at Deligrad. The Battle of Deligrad was led on September 3rd, 1806, and was another critical victory for the Serbs. Deligrad was, as we mentioned, a complex system of crude field fortifications and palisades, erected in the direct path of the "Empire Road", one of the main routes towards Istanbul, and was the main obstacle blocking the Ottoman army's route between Nish and Belgrade. In this battle the number of forces deployed was also significantly higher: the Serbian forces entrenched in the fortifications numbered roughly 34,000 men, compared to 55,000 of opposing Ottoman troops. The Ottoman forces tried repeatedly to destroy the Deligrad complex, with continuous devastating attacks that lasted close to 6 weeks. However, firmly rooted in place, the Serbs managed to repulse all of them, causing immense casualties all the while. Then, when the Turks decided to blockade the entrenched army, the Serbs succeeded in performing a series of advantageous maneuvers that broke the blockade and forced the Ottomans into full retreat. This was followed by a Serbian counter-offensive that won the Battle of Deligrad. Once again, the Ottoman forces suffered indescribable casualties, unseen up to that point in the Uprising: they left more than 30,000 soldiers dead at Deligrad, while the Serbs suffered 3,000 casualties in total. The combined victories at Deligrad and Mišar were the wind at the Serbian backs, and gave them the much needed upper-hand. Soon after, the Ottomans were forced to seek peace.

The Shifting Politics of Europe

The Fight Goes On

WHEN THE PEACE OF PRESSBURG of 1805 forced Austria to return Dalmatia to the French, it quickly became clear that this new change would not pass without crises. By losing these regions, Austria was also losing its crucial military frontier along with the seasoned Serb and Croat "grenzer" troops stationed there. Also, the Catholic element of Dalmatia was very conservative and loyal to the church, especially the common, hard-working Catholics of the region, who were mostly ethnic Croats. Amongst this Catholic element in Dalmatia, a great dissatisfaction with the revolutionary aspirations of French activists and friends grew, and was politically expressed in the sympathy for Austria and her "apostolic" majesty. The animosity amongst the Orthodox populace of the region (mostly ethnic Serbs) was not much less. Even so, those "grenzer" troops that up to that point fought on Austria's side, were now under Napoleon's flag - and fought equally well and reliably. For the developments in Serbia, where the Uprising was now a major conflict, this animosity towards the French rule played a crucial role. Since Russia was now a big enemy of Napoleon, its sphere of influence and interest was once more firmly rooted in the Balkans - where its leverage and pressures were very much needed. Furthermore, by occupying Dalmatia, the French could penetrate way deeper into the Danubian provinces at any given time - threatening Russia from a new direction. All of these events precipitated the beginning of the Russo-Turkish War of 1806-1812: Bolstered by the recent Russian defeat at Austerlitz, and leaning heavily onto Napoleon's support, the

Ottomans deposed two pro-Russian governors in Moldavia and Wallachia - Ottoman provinces on the Russian border. In order to combat this threat, the Russian Empire sent a 40,000 strong force into these regions to protect its borders, which in turn prompted the Ottomans to declare war on them. All of this had a big influence on the developments in Serbia.

Formally, this fresh war between Russia and the Ottoman Empire was declared on December 18th, 1806. At that time, a prominent Serb diplomat, Petar Ičko was in Constantinople, sent there by the Serbian command as an envoy. Ičko was sent there in the summer of 1806, in order to negotiate a peace with the Ottomans, after a string of decisive Serbian victories in the prior months. Several key requests were demanded from the Sublime Porte: a greater autonomy for the Serbs in the Belgrade Pashalik, who would still remain subjects of the Sultan, and keep paying taxes. However, they would protect their own borders and pay those taxes to the officials sent directly from Constantinople. Moreover, the *janissaries* and all other corrupt Ottoman officials that were the root of all problems - were to be expelled from the region for good. Petar Ičko (*Peter Ichko*) proved himself a shrewd diplomat, expertly utilizing the two major Serb victories at Mišar and Deligrad, as well as the newly emerged crisis between Russia and the Ottomans, to force the Sublime Porte to agree to Serbian proposals. Porta agreed to confirm everything that was promised in the agreement, and he in turn promised that the Serbs would return Belgrade to their rule. However, it was now all too late for an effective peace. If the matter had been honestly settled earlier, perhaps the Serbian Uprising could have been calmed substantially, but after the Serbian successes and the new political situation, the Serbs simply had too much of an upper hand - and an initiative that could not be easily halted. Another crucial issue emerged: the peace that Ičko got was never official - no documents were signed, and the peace remained merely an Ottoman promise: one that the Serbian leadership could not rely on. Moreover, the new developments in Moldavia and Wallachia gave them a new insight. The Russians now understood the necessity to have the Serbs as allies in this new conflict, and no longer advised the Serbian command to lay low: instead they instigated the continuation of the Uprising, with promises of help. Thus it was that when the Serbs had to decide for either an unreliable peace with the Ottomans or for a continued struggle with the Russians at their side, the answer seemed crystal clear. The Uprising against the Ottomans continued in earnest, and with a renewed zeal.

Soon after but before the end of 1806, the Russian Empire sent the Serbs financial aid to purchase ammunition and military supplies. This was followed by an official "first contact" between the Russian and Serbian forces, when on January 11th 1807, the commander of the Russian forces in Moldavia and Bessarabia, Ivan Ivanovich Mikhel'son, addressed them with an invitation to cooperate: "If we are joined together, what great deeds can we achieve?" His first suggestion was that the Serbs advance and conquer Vidin, apparently with the intention of strengthening the right wing of the Russian army there. *"The Serbian nation is worthy of being the people who are ashamed to pay tribute to the Ottomans."* he wrote. *"Would it not be better to utilize that money - which would be given to taxes - to benefit your people and the uprising against the Ottoman oppression?"*

Soon after, Karađorđe focused his attention on Belgrade - the beating heart of the Ottomans in the Balkans. Bolstered by the recent developments, he positioned his troops even closer to the city, and on November 30th, 1806, began an all out attack on the fortified town. The Serb army boasted some 25,000 soldiers, and 40 cannons. The latter were spread on five separate locations outside of the city, providing adequate bombardment in support of the troops streaming into the town. The soldiers were spread into four columns, each one directed to one of the four city gates. Karađorđe opted for a night attack and as silently as possible. The Turks in Belgrade were undoubtedly numerically superior, and also boasted an array of roughly

280 cannons. However, the Serbian attack came as somewhat of a surprise, and the city was quickly infiltrated. At 10 o'clock in the morning, after an all-night battle, Belgrade was triumphantly liberated by the Serbs which came as a big blow for the Ottomans. By December 27th, the last struggling Ottoman presence in the topmost fortress of Belgrade was quelled, and the city completely in Serb hands.

However, this was not the end of new hostilities: the death of the vizier of Belgrade, Suleyman Pasha, rekindled the flame of discord between the Serbs and the Ottomans. Remaining in Belgrade as an Ottoman representative, Suleyman Pasha attempted to secretly seek aid from neighboring Turkish *pashaliks*. However, Karađorđe and his men intercepted his letters. When Suleyman Pasha hastily left the city on February 23th, 1807, he was killed by the Serbs near Mirijevo, and this quickly led to them massacring other Turks in Belgrade and nearby places. These ugly scenes, an escalation of pent up anger by the long-oppressed Serbs, prevented any further cooperation with the Turks. Although the Ottomans at that time, at the insistence of the diplomatic representatives of both France and Austria, who wanted to separate the Serbs from the Russians, had agreed to some bigger concessions, the Serbs still opted for the Russians. *"You call us to an alliance and a joint war against the violent tyrant of the Christians, which we have always wanted from you and prayed from the all-merciful Creator"* the Serbs wrote to the Russians, *"We will do our best to fulfill your wise advice, and we will not spare our own blood while doing so, and all for the glory of the Slavs."*

At the session of the Serbian Governing State Council, its president, Voivode Sima Marković, made a fateful statement on March 19th: that Serbia considers itself an independent state. This fated declaration was sent as the only possible response to the Ottoman request, which demanded that the Serbs send 20,000 of their own soldiers to the Ottoman side, in order to help them in the struggle against the Russians. In March, Petar Ičko also returned from

Constantinople, bringing the news that the English were blocking Constantinople and that the fall of the capital was not far off. In the case of the capitulation of Constantinople, he claimed, it was a certainty that the independence of Serbia from the Porte was also not too far behind. All of these events, and the renewed glimmer of hope in the horizons of the future, worked to greatly boost the morale of the Serbian forces.

However, the situation amongst the Serbian leaders was not ideal. Experience in centuries of sporadic guerilla warfare as *"hayduks"*, led by semi-independent warband leaders, left the Serbian command with little experience in leading a unified, organized state. The emphasized self-will of Serb *voivodes* (leaders) led to a lot of disagreements and mutual fights between them. Karađorđe himself was increasingly despotic in his rule, and was not willing to allow that his leadership be undermined by the self-will of his subordinate commanders. To remedy this situation, once more the Serbs looked to Russia. In 1807, the chief Serbian diplomat and one of the most important national leaders, Prota Mateja Nenadović returned from Russia with a plan to establish an administrative body, a "council", which would have to regulate the country's administration to some extent and limit the arbitrariness of the regional leaders. This council followed the established Russian model of rule. However, several of the voivodes saw this as a suitable chance to limit Karađorđe's ever-increasing power. Karađorđe, on the other hand, seeing that the proposal was coming from Nenadović - a man influential and trusted - thought that something bigger was hiding behind the idea, and thus accepted it with reservations. Soon enough, at an assembly, in the presence of all Serb chiefs, it was concluded that the *"Governing Council of Serbia"* (Правителствующїй совѣт сербскїй) was to be established, for which each region had to send one representative. The seat of that Council was moved several times, until it settled in Smederevo and then Belgrade. Mateja Nenadović became its first president.

In early 1807, the chief Russian diplomat, and agent for the Revolutionary Serbia, Konstantin Rodofinikin, arrived amongst the Serbs. From the get go it became clear that Rodofinikin sought to side with the opponents of Karađorđe, supporting the limiting of his power. However, military aid from Russia was still nowhere to be seen in substance, and this caused great worry amongst the Serbian command which depended on it.

From the Serbian point of view, the cooperation with the Russians did not fulfill even remotely the hope and trust that the Serbs placed in it. The bulk of the Russian army was engaged in heavy fighting with Napoleon, and its actions in the Balkans were, as a direct result, of a completely secondary importance. The Serbs, lacking enough substantial information about the European situation, interpreted Russia's restraints, as the unwillingness of the Russian command to assist the Serbian forces. Karađorđe himself, well known as an impulsive man, but also as a man who had a realistic grasp on the overall situation, could not hide his dissatisfaction. He openly told the Russian command how their inactivity had placed the Serbs in a very unsuitable position. Due to previous Russian advice and promises, Serbia had rejected the Ottoman offers of an agreement, which were favorable and allowed for peace; because of their alliance with Russia, Serbia also attracted the enmity of the Austrian court, which completely closed the border and deprived the Serbian army and people of any possibility of importing food and ammunition. Karađorđe's attitude was wrongly understood as hostile towards the Russians; mostly due to his impulsive persona and his grim demeanor. In truth, he was simply aware of the fact that inactivity - especially an inactive alliance - could quickly become the undoing of his efforts in the war.

Nevertheless, after continued pressures, and the developments in the Russo-Turkish war, the Russian forces finally arrived in Serbia. Two major armies were engaged in Serbia: one was a corps under the command of the seasoned General-Major of the Don Cossack Army, Ivan Ivanovich Isaev; while the other was a contingent under the command of Lieutenant-General Ioseph Kornilovich O'Rourke (Joseph Cornelius O'Rourke).

This led to renewed offensives against the Ottomans in Serbia, beginning in the late Spring of 1807. Milenko Stojković, one of the most skilled Serbian commanders, led the offensives towards the east, with conflicts erupting close to the town of Negotin, and some Serbian forces reaching as far as Vidin. However, Milenko Stojković's forces were soon surrounded by a superior Ottoman force, and had to hold out against all odds. This developed in two successive battles, of Štubik and Malajnica, which were the most important engagements of 1807.

Surrounded at a fortified position at the Štubik Hill, Stojković desperately held off repeated Ottoman attacks and a lengthy encirclement. However, he managed to hold out long enough for Karađorđe to arrive alongside General-Major Isaev and his Russian troops. This combined Serbo-Russian army proceeded to decisively defeat the Ottomans on July 1st, 1807, at the Battle of Malajnica. In a great display of Slavic brotherhood, this army devastated the entrenched Ottoman positions, delivering great casualties and securing their first joint victory.

Soon after, the combined Serbo-Russian army under commander O'Rourke - a veteran from the battles of Austerlitz and Leipzig - won a string of victories in southeastern Serbia. It is important to note here that Joseph Cornelius O'Rourke equipped and assembled his own regiment - at his own expense - and led his force into Serbia. These forces liberated the cities of Bela Palanka, Jasika, Prahovo, and Sokobanja, and won a decisive victory in the Battle of Varvarin at the later stages of the uprising.

Now, it is time for us to shift our attention away from the battles of the Uprising, and to instead focus on the intrigues and developments on a larger political scale - in order to understand in earnest the effects that the First Serbian Uprising had on the neighboring major powers. At this point it was becoming a contested focal point where all major players of the Napoleonic Wars had to have their say: Austria, France, Russia, and the Ottoman Empire - all at the expenses of the tiny Slavic nation that was Serbia.

Things at the royal court of the Ottoman Empire were not going smoothly. Their Sultan, Selim III, was almost entirely under the influence of the French, and relied heavily on his standing with Napoleon.

Ultimately, the continued cooperation of Selim III with the French became his demise and cost him not only the throne, but his life as well. Feeling that he could not successfully quell the revolts in the Balkans and wage a successful war with the Russians, the Sultan showed an open desire to ask for French military mediation. These events and the general instability in Istanbul, led to the coups of 1807-1808, in which the revolting janissaries, alongside many of the courtiers, overthrew Selim III on May 15, 1807. They promptly placed his cousin, Mustafa IV, on the throne as the new Sultan. Shortly afterwards, Selim was assassinated. The message of the new sultan was thoroughly different, and clearly indicated that the Turks did not need French help.

Elsewhere, due to the great disappointment with his allies, especially after the heavy defeat that Napoleon inflicted on him at Eylau, The Russian Tsar Alexander decided to make peace with the French. Napoleon reluctantly accepted the offer, and so on June 25th, 1807, a treaty was concluded in Tilsit. The Treaty of Tilsit began an alliance between these two empires that virtually left the rest of continental Europe powerless. The agreement also provided for the eventual cessation of hostilities between Russia and Turkey, and also for the withdrawal of the Russian armies from Wallachia and Moldavia, a great factor that affected the developments of the Serbian Uprising. However, Serbs and their situation were nowhere distinctly mentioned in any of the treaties or negotiations.

All the while, the Serbian Uprising was received with increasing and hard to contain enthusiasm all across the lands where there was a Serbian populace - which was well beyond the borders of the Belgrade Pashalik. It was a struggle that gained a lot of momentum, and the increasingly greater victories of the Serbs were the welcomed news that spread further and further. Serbs from across the borders - from the lands of Austria, Montenegro, and elsewhere, sent aid in whatever way was possible. Also, numerous high-ranked Serb officers and soldiers crossed from the Austrian army and across the river into Serbia, while others helped the insurgents in other ways. The sympathies of the Serbs from the Srem and Banat provinces of the Austrian frontier were public and gave a lot of material to various Austrian suppliers and too zealous authorities. Certain merchants from Zemun and Mitrovica (both within Austria but close to the border) came into direct contact with the Serbian freedom fighters, supplying them with weapons, ammunition and other key necessities. However, the First Serbian Uprising had another important aspect: it was a big influence on other oppressed Serbs across the regions, giving them the needed boost of confidence to voice their own displeasure - and in some places: rise up in arms. As early as the beginning of 1807 certain Austrian authorities reported on the suspicious and "growingly dangerous" moods of Serbs in the Banat region. The same sentiment was shared also by Orthodox Romanians and the Wallachian populace. They not only insulted the "Swabians" and Hungarians, but also sent their men to the Russian military camps in Wallachia, asking the Russians to accept them into service. Furthermore the successes of Serbia's freedom fighters had revived an old hope for the renewal of the unified Serbian state, which everyone longed for. Such a state would unite the fragmented Serbian peoples which lived in several states at that point. In response to these restless spirits in Austria, the emperor and the archdukes Charles and Ludwig all issued strict orders for officials to monitor all suspicious movements and connections amongst their Serbian subjects. That only helped to a certain extent. The enthusiasm across the Serbian lands could not be easily contained. There were even reports from Lika and other regions of the Austrian frontier (in modern day Croatia) about the popular sympathies for Serbs and Russians and about the increasingly heard voices that advocated for "the creation of a Slavic or Orthodox state."

These sentiments at last spilled over into another uprising, this time on Austrian soil. This uprising broke out in the Srem (Syrmia) region, in the area directly north of Belgrade, at the end of March 1807. One of its most prominent leaders was Teodor Avramović (Теодор Аврамовић), known as Tican. The uprising is today known as *Tican's Rebellion* (Тицанова Буна) and was launched against the increasingly oppressive feudal rule in the Ruma and Illok counties, and it quickly turned into a true revolt for the rights of the impoverished peasants. Lasting roughly from April 1st to April 13th of 1807, the rebellion quickly spread over 45 villages in Syrmia and included around 15,000 peasants under arms with their center being the Voganj (Вогањ) village. Later investigation revealed that this uprising was greatly prompted by the events unfolding further south in the Serbian Uprising, and that the ultimate goal was not only the end of feudal oppression, but also the unification of Syrmia with the rest of the Serbs south of Belgrade. Throughout the short uprising, the Syrmian rebels were in direct contact with Karađorđe - mainly through one of his most important commanders, Luka Lazarević. However, the Tican's Rebellion never got the chance to grow into a bigger conflict that could unite it with the First Serbian Uprising. The Austrian military authorities took vigorous and swift measures and the uprising was quickly quelled. A major force was sent to the region, and one of the main leaders of the rebellion, Teodor Avramović Tican, was caught, imprisoned, and eventually executed on the breaking wheel. Ultimately, the Austrian emperor pardoned all the rebels except the executed Tican. Some of the main leaders fled across the river to Serbia, there to join the main uprising.

Although often overlooked or dismissed as insignificant, Tican's rebellion is important in many aspects, and we need to mention it fully here. Although lasting only a few days, this small uprising left a pretty big impression on the Austrian government and the oppressed peasants of Syrmia. After the uprising Austria paid a lot more attention to the developments in this region, especially on the communications between the Serbs in this region and those further south, across the river. The influence that the Serbs from Serbia - which was by then fully enveloped in the uprising - had on the impoverished Serb peasants from Syrmia was becoming clear, and their revolutionary ideologies were quickly spreading. Austria, of course, wanted to contain this rebellious spread and eliminate it in its roots, and thus basically became an enemy of the Serbian Revolution, considering it an entirely bad influence on its Christian servants, especially those in Syrmia. And even though Tican's Rebellion was quelled in just a few days with minimal casualties, the fight of the oppressed peasants continued - albeit in different ways. They often deserted from Austrian ranks - both singularly and en-masse - relied on mass writing of complaints, voiced criticism of the increasing feudal tyranny, and in other ways voiced their displeasure. The Austrians knew that this could again spill over into an uprising, especially if the contact with the First Serbian Uprising was to continue. That is why Austria began systematically increasing the numbers of its military in Syrmia, considering the military presence as the strongest argument that would have the best effect on the peasants. However, this made things only worse. It was repeatedly stated in Austrian sources that the "Slavic peasants of Syrmia" are "ever ready to rise up in arms", always waiting for a favorable time for an uprising. Several prominent Austrian officials claimed that such a rebellious spirit amongst the Serbs is fueled by both Russian and Serbian propaganda, as well as the talks and ideas that were brought by the veterans from wars with Napoleon. Since there was an increased threat of Serbs in Syrmia following the example of their brothers under

Ottoman rule, the Austrian military presence increased even more. In the end, this did work to limit the extent of the communications between the two sides and to contain further possibility of a new uprising in Syrmia.

This all led to the fact that Austria followed the events in Serbia with great suspicion. They considered the re-emergence of Russian influence in Serbia to be detrimental to their own interests, and even more so was the French-Russian agreement after Tilsit. Austrians then surrounded all important Serb figures with spies, not only in Serbia but in Austria as well, especially the frontier regions. Not even the most important figures were spared. Naturally, Karađorđe was given the most attention. Then, when Karađorđe sent a request to Archduke Charles on January 10, 1808, to allow him the secret export of ammunition, an idea arose amongst the Austrians - which had appeared before - that the Serbs, as a sign of loyalty, should surrender the Belgrade fortress to Austria.

Thus, regarding these matters, on February 6 instructions were given to General Baron Simbshen, the commanding officer in Petrovaradin fortress, to start negotiations with the Serbs. Karađorđe himself, even before the matter arose, wanted a meeting with Baron Simbshen, mostly due to his growing dissatisfaction with the Russian aid. Both he and Mladen Milovanović, one of his chief voivodes, said that they would be willing to put themselves - and Serbia - under the protection of Austria, provided that they were organized as a Military Frontier and that they would never be annexed to Hungary. In Vienna, they immediately accepted this proposal and planned everything that was necessary for the taking of Belgrade. These efforts were personally led by Archduke Charles, and the emperor was only subsequently informed. On March 23, Karađorđe and Simbshen met at a meeting near Belgrade. Karađorđe placed particular emphasis on the matter of Austria opening the border so that Serbs could receive food and ammunition. They were also looking for cannons and skilled artillerymen. *"If Austria comes through with these requests, the Serbs will be ready to go to Constantinople with its army"* Karađorđe spoke enthusiastically on this occasion, emphasizing that he wanted to appear as strong and confident as possible to the Austrians, in order to make his situation appear as better as possible. This was almost crucial for the Serbian army. Moreover, Karađorđe told General Simbshen that the Viennese government should not ask the Serbs to reconcile with the Ottomans or stave off their war efforts, until they liberated Nish and other Serbian regions in the south. The exact nature behind this statement of his is unclear, but in any case, the entire negotiations with the Austrians aroused the greatest doubts on the Russian side. However, it is important to note here that he did not hide these negotiations from the Russians: what is more, he informed the Russian agent Rodofinikin about all the main points, if not all the details in general. Skillful and resourceful, Rodofinikin sensed the danger of Russian influence and devised a trap. He met with Karađorđe in Topola and advised him to ask Simbshen for a written invitation. Indeed, on April 22nd, Simbshen sent Karađorđe a written invitation to come to Petrovaradin, where *"things of great importance for the Serbian people would be determined"*. That letter was then sent by Rodofinikin to the Russian authorities, as a part of his trap. The Russian ambassador in Vienna, based on this letter, demanded an explanation from the Austrian government, which thus found itself in considerable trouble. During that time, Archduke Ludwig came to *Zemun* (just north of Belgrade), presumably with the intention of bringing the issue to an end. When Karađorđe refrained from meeting him in person and when he subsequently refused negotiations on the surrender of Belgrade and the reception of the Austrian protectorate on May 18th, the Austrians began to carry out certain military demonstrations as a show of power. As an answer to this, the Serbs gathered their army along the border and prepared to meet any threat. Their written answer to the Austrians was now promptly changed, and stated that they expected a solution to their issue only from Russia and France. Rodofinikin's trap was complete, and worked in the favor of the Russians, cementing their influence in Serbia. The Serbs remained clearly and openly attached to Russia; Austria and General Simbschen were compromised; but Karađorđe, after these failed negotiations, had his reputation with the Austrian authorities almost completely ruined. The Austrians would never forget or forgive this slight.

After these events unfolded, Karađorđe made certain attempts to improve his position towards Russia. Therefore, in the fall of 1808, he started carrying out certain constitutional reforms, since the earlier draft did not receive the approval of the Russian court. Ever since the earlier establishment of the General Council, the First Serbian Uprising gained a distinct character of a successful war for liberation, and Serbia gained the first outlines of a principality free of Ottoman rule. The new constitutional act was published on December 14th, and it was a determined expression of Karađorđe's power at that time. According to this constitution, Karađorđe, with his legal descendants, was recognized "*as the first and supreme Serbian leader*", and the "*People's Council*" was given the significance of the Supreme Court. The second point expressed that "*all orders will be issued by Karađorđe through the People's Council and in agreement with the People's Council.*" This act was drawn up without the participation of Karađorđe's opposition, by his close friends and associates. Thus, the opposition in Serbia was not satisfied with this new act from the first moment it was made, finding that it was too hastily assembled and that it was declared so suddenly.

A Struggle for Survival

New Offensives of 1809

FROM THE BEGINNING of 1809, the political situation in Europe had changed significantly. Austria entered the war with Napoleon and focused all of its attention to that end. Russia was preparing for new engagements with the Ottomans as it did not find a way to regulate its relations with it on a more solid basis. On the news that England had made an alliance with the Ottoman Empire against Russia and France, Tsar Alexander decided on new and open hostilities. The Serbs, of course, remained sided with the Russians. During a mostly calm period lasting roughly a year, the Serbian command made plans for new offensives that were broadly based and with major momentum. A Serbian offensive in all directions was the general idea. Also, one of the most important Serbian goals was to unite with Montenegro. Together, they would not only achieve the unification of two smaller Serbian military forces and two Serbian populations living apart, but would, in addition to a huge morale boost, also bring the separation of Bosnia and Herzegovina from its direct ties with the Ottoman Empire, essentially cutting it off and greatly weakening the Ottoman power in the Balkans. This difficult and great task was entrusted to Karađorđe personally, who although increasingly gaining opponents, was still a seasoned commander with a string of victories behind him. The Serbs were also encouraged by a new janissary uprising in Constantinople, in the autumn of 1808, about which news were quickly spread and which confirmed the hope that the Ottomans would not be able to develop as great an army as before.

1809 was the year that brought new and renewed offensives for the Serbian army. Karađorđe began achieving his plans of a bold and confident attack with renewed strength and resolve. Thus it was that in the early spring of 1809, four major Serbian armies went on the offensive against the Ottoman Empire: one moved towards Vidin (in modern day Bulgaria) under the leadership of the seasoned veteran Milenko Stojković; the second one marched to Nish under Miloje Petrović; the third across the Drina under Sima Marković; and the fourth major army moved towards Novi Pazar in the southwest, led by Karađorđe himself. This last army was purposefully led by Karađorđe - this direction was to connect him with the Montenegrins, and the success of the offensive was critical. The successes of all three of these first armies were small or non-existent, while Karađorđe's advance was very successful. The main aspect of this success was Karađorđe's brilliant victory in the Battle of Suvodol, which was led on June 10th, 1809, when his army clashed with a major Ottoman force under the command of Numan-Beg Mahmudbegović. Previous to the battle, Karađorđe marched his army southwards through rugged terrain, and managed to masterfully cover 110 kilometers in just seven days. After successful initial clashes near the town of Sjenica, Karađorđe and his men faced off against the Ottoman army - which consisted mainly of Albanians - in the rugged mountainous terrain of Mount Suvodol. The Serbian army numbered around 4,000 men, and faced a numerically superior Ottoman force of roughly 6,000 soldiers. In the opening stages of the battle, the weary Serbian soldiers were quickly suppressed. However, Karađorđe once more relied on his familiarity with the modern European battle tactics, arranging his threatened force into an *infantry square* formation, which was a highly effective tactic of the Napoleonic Era and provided good defence from cavalry charges. This move saved his men and allowed them to continue the battle. After 3 hours of intense combat, the battle turned to the Serbian's favor - as their cavalry exploited the unprotected Ottoman flank, descending swiftly and causing devastating casualties. Soon after, the Ottomans - their own commander Numan-Pasha severely wounded - began an all-out panicked retreat and fled. The battle was a major victory that opened the way towards the major city of Novi Pazar, which Karađorđe and his men liberated soon after. Austrian sources reported close to 4,000 Ottoman casualties in this battle, but the more probable number is closer to 1,000. Serbs on the other hand, lost less than a 1,000 men. The effective use of modern Napoleonic tactics clearly showcased the rapid ageing of simple Ottoman tactics, and how the new developments in European warfare were quickly surpassing them. Karađorđe's previous military experience amongst the Austrians proved to be a major asset in the battles of the First Serbian Uprising.

However, although Karađorđe made immense success in the south, elsewhere things were not as good. Before he managed to capitalize on his success and to connect his force with the Montenegrins, Karađorđe received news of a major Serbian defeat close to Nish, and quickly had to move his forces in this direction in order to eliminate the Ottoman danger from the flank and the threat of encirclement.

This defeat was one of the most tragic and decisive moments of the entire First Serbian Uprising but also the most heroic. Known as the Battle of Čegar, it remains as one of the foremost sacrifices in the Serbian history but also as the turning point of the First Uprising. One of the four armies that was part of the Spring offensive of 1809, was under the command of Miloje Petrović with roughly 10,000 men. By mid May the force approached the major city of Nish, and positioned their forces into six entrenched fortifications on the surrounding hill, with one of the major trenches being on Čegar Hill, commanded by voivode Stevan Sinđelić (Стеван Синђелић). The Ottomans opposing them were commanded by Hurshid Ahmed Pasha at the head of 8,000 men, alongside Mustafa Pasha, Mahmut Pasha, and other seasoned Ottoman leaders. After initial clashes, the Ottomans received major reinforcements around May 20th, which brought their total numbers to around 30,000 men. After somewhat "probing attacks" on the first trench, the battle grew on May 31st, as the Ottoman force focused on the trench at Čegar Hill. This crucial position became severely pressured, and Stevan Sinđelić and his men became cut off from the rest of the Serbian positions. The battle that formed here is widely agreed to be one of the bloodiest in the entire First Serbian Uprising: the Ottomans made 5 consecutive all-out attacks on the Serbian positions, and were repulsed each time, with both sides suffering great casualties. It was reported in several sources that the bodies littered the trench and could be walked on. However, the numerical superiority of the Ottoman force meant that the Serbian defenders had no chance of survival. Seeing that his situation was dire, Stevan Sinđelić made a daring move. After the entire day of fighting, with the masses of the Ottoman soldiers pouring into the entrenchments, Sinđelić approached the main gunpowder magazines in the center of the fort, drew out his pistol, and blew them up. The ensuing explosion was so devastating, that the entire position and the area around it was utterly devastated. In a heroic moment, Stevan Sinđelić sacrificed his own and the lives of his men in order to take down the vast majority of the Ottoman troops. The explosion claimed thousands of lives: various reports exist, with some sources citing 10,000 dead Ottoman soldiers and 2,000 Serb soldiers; and others claiming the loss of 3,000 men on each side.

While it was a decisive defeat for the Serbs, it did land a significant blow to the Ottoman army. The rest of the Serb forces in other trenches were forced to fall back to the Deligrad redoubts, and the offensive towards Nish ultimately failed. Due to this defeat, Karađorđe had to altogether abandon his idea of reclaiming the southeastern regions of "Old" Serbia, while the Ottoman vizier of Rumelia (the Balkans) capitalized on the situation and penetrated deep into eastern Serbia, once more conquering it. Karađorđe only barely managed to organize a defense and stop further advances.

In the wake of the Battle of Čegar, the Ottoman commander, Hurshid Ahmed Pasha, angered by the loss of such a large force, ordered that the fallen Serbian soldiers of the battle be decapitated, their heads skinned, and their skulls built into a purpose built tower. This ghastly creation was erected on the main road towards Constantinople, as a warning sign to all those who attempt to rise up against the Ottoman Empire: 952 skulls, including that of Stevan Sinđelić, were built into the so-called "Skull Tower" (Ћеле Кула). It remains there to this very day, as a reminder of the heroic sacrifice of the heroes of Čegar Hill, who are - alongside their leader Stevan Sinđelić - immortalized as the eternal heroes of the Serbian nation.

Following this hard defeat, the Serbian army lost its initiative in the Uprising, which it held for so long. From that moment on, they were on the defensive. However, many historians argue that the defeat at Čegar was in many ways brought by the increasing inability of the Serbian commanders to work together and agree on the same course of action. Their self-will and growing greed created open hostilities amongst them, and this obstructed a clear and concise course of action in the offensive. It is said that by the time Karađorđe arrived to the front in the east, it was completely disorganized with several of the leaders doing what they wanted. Many claim that Sinđelić suffered a defeat and sacrificed himself due to the fact that no one wanted to help him as they were too focused on internal affairs and arguments. Nevertheless, the reputation of several key commanders, and that of Karađorđe, were all severely stained.

After this difficult crisis, Karađorđe was faced with a fateful question: he had to decide with whom to work for the benefit of his cause and his people. Russia has been slow to send more military aid, was inactive, and preoccupied with many issues in Western and Northern Europe; He resented Austria a lot, and it too suffered against Napoleon, and moreover it didn't fully trust him. In the end however, not knowing precisely the full extent of the development of events and the fights between the Austrians and the French, Karađorđe asked for the protection of Austria, returning mainly to the starting point, when negotiations were held with General Baron Simbshen. Count Heinrich von Bellegarde, Viceroy of Lombardy-Venetia and Field Marshal of Austria, wrote in the Petrovaradin Fortress that one should not believe in Serbian sincerity. Serbs are sending pleas on every side, but are "*in fact, probably looking to buy more time, to play by their own rules.*" Although these words were harsh, there is undoubtedly a lot of truth in them, as the desperate situation in Serbia made it appear increasingly so. The Serbs certainly, and understandably, looked for their benefit and in their best interests, after being so repeatedly abandoned by all major powers. On this occasion, considering the Ottoman strength and Serbia's growing weakness, Karađorđe was convinced once more that they could hardly or not at all resist the real Ottoman power on their own. This certainly made their aspirations to obtain the protection of some foreign power completely sincere.

With the Austrian assistance becoming impossible, and the Russians preoccupied and slow to react, intimidated, and not wanting to be left alone, Karađorđe decided to make offers to the French at the same time. The great victor Napoleon, who so decisively and ingeniously broke the Austrian military resistance in 1809, impressed the Serbs continually. In their distress, in the summer of that same year, they came up with the idea of asking him to accept them under his powerful protection. In agreement with the Council, they did so on August 16. The one to present the Serbian offers was Captain Rade Vučinić from Karlovac in the Kordun region of modern day Croatia. At the time Karlovac was one of the important centers of the Austrian military frontier meaning the Captain was a man with good capabilities and background to speak with such a lofty figure as the French leader. He found Napoleon in Vienna, just as he was preparing to return back to France. In a meeting, Rade Vučinić relayed the offers sent by Karađorđe that the French forces enter Serbian cities and be garrisoned by them, an option that Austria desired from him earlier. The Serbs promised that they would be loyal allies to the French, not only those Serbs in Serbia, but also in all other regions where they lived. The Serbs emphasized that they could be of use to the French in their fight against Austria. The Serbian offer was delivered to Napoleon himself, but he could not accept it due to his obligations to the Ottoman Empire. Nevertheless he emphasized that he could not remain indifferent *"to the fate of a nation that has shown so much perseverance and courage."* Therefore, an order was issued to the French vice consul in Bucharest to maintain ties with the Serbs, but in the greatest secrecy. This was of little consolation to Karađorđe.

At the same time, Serbs were looking to improve their original relations with the Russians. Rodofinikin's previous intrigues and meddling in internal affairs was recognized as a wrong move on both sides, and the situation could be improved. Therefore, the Serbian leader sent letters and envoys to the Russian headquarters, directly to the famed Prince Bagration, to warn of the bias of these reports and to plead his case once again, in a renewed light.

The Russians, who strengthened their influence in the Balkans with a pre-planned motive, saw for themselves that the growing Serbian dissatisfaction was not entirely without their fault, and they made honest attempts to fix it. On both the Russian and Serbian side, there arose a sincere desire for relations to be returned to the original state. The new Russian commander-in-chief, Count Mikhail Fedotovich Kamensky, contributed immensely to that end. He also sought to calm down the quarreling Serbian leaders and made attempts to secure Karađorđe and his leadership. Thus it was that in 1810, a renewed Russian military presence in Serbia appeared, this time led by the prominent Lieutenant General Count Joseph Cornelius O'Rourke (Ioseph Kornilovich O'Rourke), a Russian nobleman of Irish ancestry.

In 1810, Karađorđe took upon himself the most difficult task for his army - to attempt and improve the military position on the Morava

River and thus prevent further Ottoman penetration from the direction of Nish. However, the Ottomans changed the main direction of their advance and, bypassing the fortified positions at Deligrad, struck from the direction of the city of Kruševac, from where it was easier to penetrate into the central Serbian region of Šumadija. The disorganized Serbian companies, disheartened by the previous year's failures, were quite discouraged and many left their positions in hopes of protecting their families. However, it was at this point that the newly arrived Russian army was of great help. Reliable leadership, several thousand Russian troops, military supplies and aid, as well as the direct involvement of the Russian General Field Marshal Kutuzov, was a much needed help to boost Serbian hopes. Soon enough, this joint Serbo-Russian army scored a fresh and decisive victory against the Ottoman forces. This occurred at the Battle of Varvarin, between 18th and 20th September 1810. The joint forces of the Serbs and the Russians, commanded by O'Rourke, awaited the Turks at a strategic point close to the Morava River, the place where the Ottoman advances from the Nish direction *had* to be stopped. Once more, the Ottomans were commanded by Hurshid Ahmed Pasha, who - yet again - had the numerical superiority: he had 15,000 troops against a smaller force of roughly 1,000 Serbs and Russians. Nevertheless, the superior tactics, and a favorable position on the open fields at Varvarin, allowed the Serbo-Russian army to withstand the Ottoman attacks. Once more, the key formations of the Napoleonic Era were a decisive factor: O'Rourke - himself a seasoned commander from the Battle of Austerlitz - arranged his forces into infantry squares, and relied on precise cannon fire support. The Ottomans suffered a decisive defeat, losing over a thousand men.

Interestingly Karađorđe was not present in the Varvarin Battle, as O'Rourke advised, and almost insisted that he should not be present. He reportedly stated that *"should the Turks win the battle (as their numerical superiority was a known fact) it is better that they defeat only me, rather than both of us."* However, it is most likely that O'Rourke insisted solely for the reason to have unobstructed command of the battle - which itself is an understandable fact. His experience could not be challenged, and he needed independence in this decisive battle.

Almost immediately after the securing of this right flank, Karađorđe hurried to the west, to the River Drina, where the Serbian forces were threatened by a massive Ottoman army that moved in from Bosnia. At his side, Karađorđe also had 300 Russian cossacks. Arriving with this force close to the town of Loznica near the Drina River, Karađorđe and a force of roughly 1,200 fighters managed to repel a much larger Ottoman army at the Battle for Loznica. Known also as the Battle of Tičar, it was fought between 17th and 18th of October, 1810. The Ottoman army was commanded by Ali-Pasha Vidajić, and numbered approximately 30,000 men. The Serbs facing them were in fortified positions, and numbered 1,200 men at first, but this number rose to 10,000 with quick arrival of additional reinforcements. The ensuing battle was claimed by most to be one of the largest clashes in the First Serbian Uprising, with Karađorđe himself saying that it was the biggest battle they had thus far. In the end, the Ottomans were repelled and defeated, and thus Karađorđe managed to secure his left flank as well.

Between the Hammer and the Anvil
A Gradual Downfall

THINGS WERE SOON GOING to turn for the worse in Serbia. Once more affected by the overall political developments in Europe, the Serbs again lost the support from major powers. At the end of 1810 and onwards, things were not developing well for Russia. With the might of Napoleon being ever increasing, and the possibility of a French Invasion of Russia being all too real, Russia had it in its own interests to seek peace and to remove its military presence from Serbia much to the dismay of the desperate Serbian fighters. Ultimately, this did occur and the Russians withdrew from Serbia amidst complex political events. With the signing of the Peace of Bucharest in 1812, and the peace between the Russians and the Ottoman Empire, the Serbs were effectively left to fend for themselves yet again. Moreover, this second Russian retreat from Serbia came at the pinnacle of Karađorđe's power and at the moment when the Serbian expectations were the highest. Other difficulties weighed down the Serbian governing body. Karađorđe's opposition grew amongst the regional leaders, and now he even had open enemies and opponents. Self-will was rampant, as was the inability of the leaders to agree on the due course of action, and the growing separation between proponents for Austrian or Russian aid. In an attempt to control those powerful commanders that were his opponents, Karađorđe made the decision to bring them into the General Council (Совјет), as ministers in the government. The two commanders in question were some of the most seasoned veterans and finest heroes in the Uprising, Petar Dobrnjac and Milenko Stojković. Both of them refused to accept the position, and amidst complex internal affairs and a fight with Karađorđe, they were sentenced and exiled from the country. Their exile caused mass displeasure amongst the people. While everyone realized that they were wilful and wouldn't accept orders easily, they were nevertheless the heroes of the Uprising, and able and seasoned military commanders. Later historians perfectly summed this wrong move: when Karađorđe removed his two best commanders, he left an open path for the Turks to march back in. Also, as much as Karađorđe was a natural born warrior - a skilled military commander - he was also rather unskilled in political matters and intrigues. A man with a strong temperament, he was also susceptible to act on first impressions and could be influenced by others, on many occasions hesitating in diplomatic moves and accepting the reluctant suggestions that were given to him, only if they seemed to be able to yield a successful result.

The Treaty of Bucharest that ended the conflicts between the Russians and the Ottoman Empire, had one small mention of Serbia. It was the last effort the Russians made to aid Serbia in its plight: the article number 8 of the treaty stated that the Turks are to return to Serbia and garrison the cities there, and to destroy any Serb fortifications made up to that point; in return, the Ottomans agreed to give total amnesty and a certain degree of self rule to the Serbs. However, the Serbs had no idea what was agreed in Bucharest for a long time. The Russians said nothing and kept them somewhat in the dark. Moreover, the Russian agents in Serbia were given direct orders not to explicitly mention the Article 8 of the treaty, and only speak of it in vague terms. Only when the Turks re-entered Serbia did the Serbian command learn of the Bucharest treaty and its contents. The Serbs realised what had happened as the situation unfolded rapidly and felt deep disappointment. This severely affected morale, especially with the withdrawal of Russian troops from Serbia, and then from Moldavia and Wallachia. All of these events were ominous portents of a looming defeat.

From the very beginning of the new offensives against Serbia in 1812, the Ottomans were ready to negotiate with the Serbs, if not with the intention of accepting all of their conditions, then at the very least to listen to them and find a solution that would be suitable for both sides. But this attitude quickly changed when they saw the increased Serbian hesitation and Russia's difficult situation with the looming invasion by Napoleon. This, and the suggestions made by main Russian opponents, made the Ottomans quickly change their viewpoint. Serbian deputies were sent to Nish, with little prospect of success. As the first condition for negotiations, in the spirit of the eighth article of the Bucharest treaty, and as a proof of the good will of the Serbs, the Ottomans demanded that the Serbs let the Turkish army into their cities and to hand over all cannons and all weapons. The Ottomans were not willing to waste any time in overly long negotiations, and they also wanted to promptly remove the entire Serbian issue from the agenda while Russia was busy with Napoleon. The energetic Hurshid Ahmed Pasha, well known to the Serbs from the offensives of 1809, now became the Ottoman Grand Vizier (prime minister) in August 1812, and demanded quick decisions and action. His concessions to the Serbs were getting fewer and fewer. The "insurgents" - as the Ottomans called them - were first asked to surrender the cities as a sign of good will, and he then demanded that they first of all obey and accept what little was given to them. The Serbs initially sought self-government, but the Ottomans immediately refused to recognize their *kingdom within an empire.* The harder the Ottoman pressures became, the softer and more discouraged the Serbs were. The Russian advice and pressures in Constantinople that worked for the benefit of the Serbs were almost non-existent, and slowed down the Turkish extreme measures only by a fraction, but in the end they could not significantly change the Serbian destiny at that time. All the while, the Ottomans closely watched the developments in Europe before making a move against the Serbs. When the so-called *Armistice of Pläswitz* occurred in June 1813, which brought a nine-week truce between Napoleon and the Allied Powers, the Ottomans feared that the Russians would briefly return their attention towards the Serbian question. Thus they decided to act before this could happen, and to solve the matter for good. At the beginning of July 1813, according to a plan prepared in advance, three major Turkish armies set out for Serbia: one from Vidin, another from Nish, and the third one from the west, across the River Drina.

The Serbian position was difficult to say the least. Alone, without any allies, scarce with ammunition, and severely affected by internal quarrels, their morale had collapsed before the first fight began. Now an universal belief was held that they could not sustain themselves without reliance on any major power. As it quickly become a reality, it brought ravaging fear. The real enthusiasm for the fight that characterized their early triumphs now disappeared. Karađorđe himself was no longer the same man. The struggle with both external and internal enemies has greatly exhausted his patience, his nerves, his strength and momentum. The original zeal was slowly dissipating from him, and the pressures of the Uprising were becoming too great to bear. He had long been overwhelmed by doubts about the outcome of his cause and was becoming poisoned by distrust that settled in the people. Even before the Ottoman attack, on March 30, 1813, anticipating defeat, Karađorđe asked for permission to move to Russia. In the summer he also fell ill, apparently from typhus, in the most difficult days when his presence was necessary to lift the spirits and enlighten the people. He lay sick in Topola and wilted more and more, both physically and morally. It is claimed that in July of 1813 he suffered a nervous breakdown after an argument with one of his main commanders over the defense of the country.

The Ottomans made swift progress in this decisive and renewed offensive. The sheer amount of troops they mustered was the clear insight into the nature of the attack: one final effort to smite the Serbian resistance once and for all. All together their armies numbered roughly 250,000 men descending onto the impoverished Serbian forces in one fell swoop. The Serbs made attempts at organizing a defense, but with little success. The first major defeat came to them at the Battle of Ravnje in Zasavica, near the town of Šabac, in August 1813. This battle lasted for roughly 17 days and was one of the largest clashes up to that point noted for how bloody it was. Here, the French assistance to the Ottomans was great. They gave aid in forms of artillery, and instructed the Turks in trench and tunnel building. In the end, the severely outnumbered Serb defenders were beaten with heavy losses. It was here that the noted Jovan Gligorijević laid his life. He and his unit of 300 fighters sacrificed themselves in order to guard the retreat of the bulk of the Serbian force. They fought to death.

In the east too, a major defeat was suffered. Fierce battles erupted around the city of Negotin, which suffered a lengthy siege. Its outnumbered garrison could not hold against the fierce Ottoman onslaught, and it was ultimately defeated. One of the major Serbian heroes and commanders died here - hajduk Veljko Petrović.

By late 1813, the First Serbian Uprising was finished, finally collapsing after several years of heroic fighting. Seeing the situation and realizing the fact that all was lost, Karađorđe - in agreement with his close advisors - decided to leave the country. On Sunday, September 21st 1813, he crossed over the Danube and first fled into Zemun, and then further north to the Fenek Monastery - both then in Austria. All major Serbian commanders, voivodes, and leaders also left the country - all except one: voivode Miloš Obrenović, of whom we shall speak soon.

This collapse of the uprising was undoubtedly a heavy blow for all Serbs. But to many it was clear that this blow was only temporary and served as a difficult lesson. In fact, in many ways it was needed.

The First Serbian Uprising and its collapse placed the Serbian question before Europe as an integral part of the so-called Eastern Question. Until then, no one on the sidelines cared that Serbia should be established as a separate state. However, since the First Uprising erupted and the creation of the Serbian state loomed on the horizon, that understanding was fundamentally changed. What's more, the fierce struggle of the Serbian people served as a much needed example for other oppressed nations to follow.

Although to some it seemed that the Serbian defeat in 1813 signified the loss of everything, in reality it was not so. Not only did the events of the First Serbian Uprising and its defeat awaken a renewed national consciousness amongst the Serbs, but it also placed in them an aspiration to give active resistance to tyrannical oppression.

While in Austria, the Serbian leadership was granted no favors, and was looked down with discontent, as the Austrian authorities greatly distrusted them. Karađorđe himself was detained in Graz, and desperately worked with the Russian consuls in Vienna to find a chance for his commanders and himself to find refuge in Russia. Both the Russian Tsar personally, and the Russian government, feeling some responsibility for the doomed Serbian fate, were willing to receive and take care of all Serbian refugees in their country. Austria did not like the close ties between the Serbs and Russia and after lengthy negotiations, and great involvement from the Russian government, the Serbian leaders finally received permission to go to Russia. At the end of September 1814, still clutching to the burning embers of hope, Karađorđe and his men headed on towards brotherly Russia, uncertain of the future of their own nation.

A Glorious Defeat

Was the Fight Truly Over?

THE SITUATION IN THE re-conquered Serbia was catastrophic. Ottoman reprisals were cruel and barbaric, and spared no one. Many of the previous vague promises by the Ottomans were overlooked, ignored, and straight up dismissed. The common folk was tormented, killed, and taken into slavery. As a direct result, waves of refugees fled across the Danube and into the regions of Banat and Syrmia in Austria (modern-day Serbia), hoping to save their lives.

Serbia was literally overrun - swiftly and brutally. The common folk suffered the most: many were taken into slavery, or suffered from the deadly typhus or plague epidemics that were rampant at the time. Starvation and poverty were also great. In just one day, on October 17, 1813, over 1,800 women and children were taken into slavery and brought to the market in Belgrade for sale. The exact nature of these cruel reprisals by the Ottomans can be easily deduced. The Bosnian Ottoman vizier spoke with great satisfaction to the French consul, saying that the commanders of defeated and devastated Serbia *"can no longer find people to use in a new revolt."*

However, the torment and the reprisals soon came to an end after 20 days approximately . Again, the developments on the European fronts led to the calming of Ottoman angst. The fresh news of Napoleon's great defeat at Leipzig, and of Russia's increasingly crucial role in European politics, were a sobering factor for the Ottoman government. Well aware of their obligations to Russia with regards to the Serbs, they toned down their reprisals and changed their approach.

They declared a general amnesty and even began to return to power some of the country's remaining influentials, in hopes of calming the situation and returning to square one. It is here that Miloš Obrenović comes into the story. He was amongst the most respectable and talented among the Serbian commanders that remained in Serbia. He was also one of the wealthiest. He was appointed by the Ottomans to be the governing knyaz of a big province, and quickly entered into their trust.

However, the Ottomans made a mistake when they appointed Suleyman Skopljak Pasha as the new Vizier of Belgrade. Although a very distinguished and skilled military commander, he was a man who was deeply resentful of the Serbs, and in constant conflict with them throughout the Uprising. The Ottoman government relied on his experience and shrewdness, but overlooked his vengeful nature and the long history he had with the Serbs. Soon after, this negative nature of his would come to the forefront and threatened to stir up the shaky peace that settled in Serbia.

However, from the get go, Miloš Obrenović had big plans for himself chiefly, and then for his nation. Known as a shrewd, opportunist, and crafty figure, he was quick to slander the name of Karađorđe. He, and the good part of the people, blamed Karađorđe for the defeat of the uprising, and now began analyzing all the mistakes he had supposedly made in the preceding years. It is crucial to note here that even before, while serving under Karađorđe, Obrenović was one of his opponents. Now, in the newly emerged situation, Obrenović used this fresh opportunity to come as the foremost of the Serb leaders, to fully slander Karađorđe and worked to bar him from ever returning to Serbia. By 1814, the surviving letters show that Miloš Obrenović wrote to be speaking *"in the name of the entire nation"*. However, his opportunist nature would soon come to the surface.

In September of 1814, a new, smaller uprising erupted in Serbia. It was instigated and led by an influential Serbian commander,

Hadži-Prodan Gligorijević, and became known as Hadži-Prodan's Rebellion. However, it came at a very bad moment, was poorly organized, and without a good plan. It came as a direct result of renewed oppressive Ottoman measures, and roughly lasted until December of 1814, when it was decisively quelled by the Ottomans. However, Miloš Obrenović himself fought against this new uprising. He joined his forces with the Ottoman forces, promising to help them put the rebellion down, if they promised amnesty to those involved. And although he worked against his own nation and brought to the demise of many people involved in this small uprising, his requests were altogether ignored by the Ottomans - no amnesty was given. Instead, over 300 rebels were captured, marched in shackles to Belgrade, and there executed in cruel ways, mostly by impalement on spikes. The other Serb commanders would later hold this against Obrenović.

The Flame Renewed

The Start of the Second Serbian Uprising

THIS SMALLER UPRISING was a good cause for the vengeful Suleyman-Pasha to bring about a new and brutal, oppressive rule. His new reign of terror was as much fuelled by his own fears, and also by his illogical need to solve the "Serbian question" by killing as many innocent people as possible. Things were thus, once more, getting out of hand, and his reign was becoming much alike the reign of the *dahijas* that preceded the Uprising in 1804. Several key Serbian leaders that remained in the country were killed, foremost of them being Stanoje Glavaš, whose head was displayed on the gates of Belgrade. Miloš Obrenović was also threatened.

Reports received by the Serbs in Russia and Austria during January and February 1815 were as dire as could be. Recognizing the gravity of the situation, and seeing a chance of a renewed conflict, Miloš Obrenović immediately asked in Vienna if there was any real chance of success in a new clash with the Ottomans, emphasizing the need *"to defend ourselves, and not to let so many innocent people be slaughtered and exterminated."*

Worried and afraid, and seeing that there was no longer any certainty of peaceful and non oppressed existence, people around Serbia began to think more and more about a new uprising. The general mentality declared that "if one is to die, then it is better to die in battle". Thus, secret meetings and negotiations began in March of 1815. Miloš Obrenović was under constant surveillance and was not allowed to leave Belgrade by the direct order of the Vizier. However, he managed to slip out by trickery. As soon as he left Belgrade and came to his quarters at Crnuće, he was informed about and promptly appointed the leader of the uprising. Cautious and wise, Miloš Obrenović did not want to rush the first movements and make a bad initial step. He wanted to wait for the best weather, to inform his potential allies across the border, and also to renew all crucial connections and store as much ammunition and supplies as was possible. Thus, the Second Serbian Uprising began spontaneously and almost unexpectedly. Even before Miloš managed to slip out of Belgrade, local leaders around Serbia began murdering Ottoman tax collectors and regional tyrants. Formally, these leaders and elders assembled alongside Miloš Obrenović in Takovo (Таково), on April 23rd 1815, where it was agreed to once again rise up against the Ottoman tyranny. Miloš Obrenović - although reluctant at first - was chosen as the leader of the uprising, and uttered his famous words before the assembled people: "*Here am I - and here is your war with the Turks!*"

Thus began the Second Serbian Uprising.

In many ways the Second Serbian Uprising differed than the First - mainly it was this time focused on the legal Ottoman rule, i.e. Suleyman Pasha, while the First one was directed against the rebellious *janissaries* and then grew from there. From the very start, the Ottomans were adamant at quickly quelling this new uprising and containing the Serbian threat.

The Vizier of Belgrade, Suleyman Skopljak Pasha, was the chief behind this order. He appointed his second-in-command, Caja Imshir-Pasha, and at once set him at the head of an army towards the interior of Serbia to face the "insurgents". Moreover, he was quick to close off his borders and to start rounding up and imprisoning all important people.

Imshir-pasha went straight to the town of Čačak, which was besieged by the Serbs, and attacked their trenches on the hill known as Ljubić. This grew into the fierce Battle of Ljubić (Бој на Љубићу), on June 6th 1815. The fighting over entrenched Serb positions lasted for several days, even though the Serbs did not have enough weapons. This battle was marked by the effective use of artillery by the Serbs, and was a prolonged and difficult struggle. During this battle a famous Serbian commander was killed, Tanasko Rajić, but his forces managed to rally and to inflict a defeat upon the Ottomans, who promptly retreated to the safety of the Čačak town walls. During that time, Miloš Obrenović defeated the Ottoman forces near Palež, which was a strategically crucial location due to the ferry that was located there and which allowed the Serbs to transfer ammunition and supplies more easily. Following this victory and the securing of the ferry crossing, many influential Serb leaders from the First Uprising immediately crossed over into Serbia, carrying some weapons and ammunition. Immediately afterwards, the major city of Valjevo was liberated. After these important initial successes, Miloš moved to Ljubić, taking with him two cannons, which he received from the new arrivals across the border. It was these cannons that Tanasko Rajić died defending, as they were entrusted to him. Imshir Pasha was also killed in these battles around Ljubić. His death was a big blow for the Ottomans, and the loss of his leadership quickly led them to disarray, and they hastily fled from Čačak on May 29th. A month later, after a lengthy and fierce battle, the city of Požarevac was also conquered, making for yet another triumph in the Second Serbian Uprising. These initial victories greatly boosted the morale of the people, and clearly showcased the readiness and the unyielding zeal of the Serbian freedom fighters. Often outnumbered, they still managed to fight ferociously and rack up a string of decisive victories against the Ottomans.

Seeing that the situation was once more getting out of hand, the Ottoman government sought to destroy the Serbian resistance as quickly as was possible. In order to do so, the Sublime Porte sent two armies into Serbia. The first, from the direction of Nish, was led by the Rumelian Morashli Ali Pasha, and the second, heading from the direction of Bosnia, was led by the former Great Vizier, (at the time the Bosnian Vizier) Hurshid Pasha.

Suleyman Pasha, the Vizier of Belgrade, was quickly receiving the brunt of the blame for the Uprising, from the Ottoman Government. He desperately sought to defend himself, blaming Austria for involving itself and inciting the Serbs to rebel - when this was totally untrue. In fact, Austria was not at all inclined to help the Serbs in any way; on the contrary, it caused them many difficulties.

Reminding himself of the outcome of the First Serbian Uprising, Miloš Obrenović knew that he could not make hasty and uncalculated decisions. He did not and could not expose himself too much until he saw what the development of the event would be like, and most importantly, how the outside powers would accept it. Thus it was clear that extreme care had to be applied in every aspect of the uprising, so as to not repeat the doomed fate of the first attempt. Similar to the first uprising though, he stood by his claim that Serbia was not seeking an enemy in the official Ottoman government, but was simply responding to the tyranny and oppression they suffer under Suleyman Pasha and in the Belgrade Pashalik.

Nevertheless, even with these "peaceful" claims, the conflict between the two warring sides did not subside. What's more is a new battle erupted, one of the fiercest of the few that marked the Second Serbian Uprising. Known as the Battle of Dublje (Бој на Дубљу), it was fought on July 26th 1815, and pitted the ragged and barely entrenched Serbian fighters against a strong Ottoman force under the command of Ibrahim Pasha. One of the decisive clashes of the second uprising, it came out as a decisive Serbian victory after a prolonged and bitter fight. In the battle Ibrahim Pasha was captured, but Obrenović decided to treat him with respect and to free him - perhaps as a sign of good will.

However, the armed clashes and battles of the Second Serbian Uprising lasted only around 4 months, and soon after these key defeats the Ottoman approach changed immensely. While the First Serbian

Uprising was rife with battles at every step, and was a long and bitter struggle, the second uprising did not have the same intensity and fierceness - in many ways it did not have to have them. Needless to say, the rapid developments on the European stage greatly dictated the steps that the Ottomans made. Napoleon's defeat was the big factor that caused their military actions in Serbia to come to a grinding halt. Offensives and movements were no longer conducted, and now the commanders waited. It was clear that the Ottomans feared the direct involvement and mediation of Russia now that Napoleon was out of their way.

The main reason why Constantinople wanted to avoid Russian involvement in the Serbian question was the fact that it would encourage the Serbs even further and prolong their resistance. Also, there existed the matter of the eighth article of the Bucharest Treaty, which still served as an obligation for the Ottomans.

Thus it was that after a string of devastating defeats in the first half of 1815, the Ottomans - pressured by the final defeat of Napoleon and the change in Europe's politics - decided to begin negotiations with the Serbian leader Miloš Obrenović. However, approaching these negotiations was more challenging. Now the Vizier of Bosnia, Hurshid Pasha, was much more a soldier than a diplomat. His rule was rigid and in many ways absolute, and he, a veteran of many battles against the Serbs, was known for his resentment of the Serbian people. Obrenović thus knew that negotiations with him would not end well. On the other hand, the new Vizier of Belgrade, Marashli Ali Pasha, was much more diplomatic, having a significantly better grasp of the seriousness of the situation. Where Hurshid fiercely objected to Serbs having possession of weapons of any kind, Marashli Pasha did not object to that notion whatsoever - as long as loyalty to Constantinople remained in place. Obrenović realized quite well that there was a great difference and a slight rivalry between these two Ottoman leaders, and that is where his cunning came in handy. He himself was much different than his predecessor, Karađorđe - he was much more inclined to diplomacy than to warfare. Furthermore, it was becoming clear that the question in Serbia was to be resolved with negotiations and diplomacy, rather than with continued bloodshed. Thus, the first steps towards a resolution began. A Serbian delegation was sent to Constantinople, and an Ottoman contingent allowed to enter Belgrade unopposed. Negotiations began based on the previous attempt at peace - the Ichko Treaty from 1806 - and worked from there. Marashli Ali Pasha was the one entrusted by the Ottoman Government to lead the negotiations on their part. There was still a good deal of distrust on the Ottoman side, and they didn't want to give complete independence to the Serbian people. Nevertheless, they placed themselves in a position where a certain amount of concessions had to be made. The Serbs themselves were willing to accept some measures in advance. All the agreements between Miloš Obrenović and Marashli Ali Pasha were never laid down on paper, and were entirely unwritten agreements. But even so, the success that Serbia made with these negotiations was still enormous and boosted the morale and hopes all around the nation. The country was again at peace and mostly in the hands of the Serbian people. Moreover, Obrenović gained a reputation boost and was widely accepted as the national leader with great influence. Thus it was that in the fall of 1815, the war torn Serbia could at last breathe a sigh of relief. Peace returned to the land, which was to last for a good number of years, giving the people a chance to recover and mourn their dead with a sense of satisfaction that their voices were heard and their demands met.

Nevertheless, it is important to note that the end result here was not a full independence for Serbia - but it was surely a big first step towards that end.

Serbia's self-government was based on the following terms: the Serbian people were to collect their taxes themselves; along with the Ottoman officials, all Serbs were to be judged by their own leaders as well (bringing equality and unbiased trials into the courts). In Belgrade, the Serbs got their own *"People's Office"*, as the highest administrative and judicial body, another important step. Moreover, Miloš Obrenović became the main Serbian *knyaz* (prince), meaning he had a lofty and important position alongside the Ottoman governing body.

All of this was somewhat delivered in a written form, in the so-called *firmans* (royal decree on a constitutional level) that the Ottomans brought in 1816. Although there was no mention of any self-government per se, numerous privileges for the Serbs were directly outlined. The Ottomans had a hard time admitting before the Russians and the Austrians that the Serbs won a degree of independence, and thus did not officially mention it, although in reality it was clearly seen. Thus all concessions made by them were titled as "rights". In this way the semi-independent state of the Principality of Serbia was recognized although it still had to pay a yearly tax to the Ottoman Sultan, and had to allow an Ottoman garrison in Belgrade and other "imperial" cities.

Now the time came for Obrenović to focus more on settling the internal affairs in Serbia, as there were still obstacles and oppositions that he had to solve. Although he was the most powerful man in Serbia at the time, he was not without rivals. One of his main opponents in this period was Petar Moler, an active and ambitious leader who served from 1815 as a sort of Prime Minister. He specifically requested from Miloš Obrenović for the power in the country to be shared with him and his associates. Obrenović was, of course, not a man who would easily share his immense power with others, especially not after witnessing the internal struggles and bickering that marked the First Serbian Uprising. Thus, in 1816, Petar Moler and his chief associate Melentije Nikšić, both the chief opposition to Obrenović's rule, were killed. This was followed by others who stepped up in hopes of curbing the might of Obrenović and standing in his path. In the spring of 1817, respected leaders and heroes of the First Uprising, Pavle Cukić and Sima Marković revolted against Miloš and his rule, seemingly with an aim to have Karađorđe return to Serbia. Miloš Obrenović had the revolt quickly suppressed, and both of these prominent men were executed. This was a clear insight into the nature of Obrenović's rule, and the fact that he did adopt a somewhat despotic or totalitarian rule, quickly dealing with any opposition and threat to his power. However, Karađorđe remained as his biggest rival and a viable threat to his power - as his reputation was still somewhat strong amongst the people, with many voices expressing the desire for his return to Serbia.

The End of a Great Hero
The Death of Karađorđe

KARAĐORĐE HIMSELF WAS still in Russia, and still harbored a fierce desire to entirely rid Serbia from the Ottoman pressures. However, both the Russians and Obrenović knew that his return to Serbia could potentially spell disaster for the newly found peace with the Ottomans, as a renewed conflict could undo all that was achieved up to that point. Of course, there still remained the question of how efficiently Karađorđe could lead a new fight: he was now ostensibly weaker, troubled with melancholy, and with ailing health. He also still had as many opponents as he had supporters, and his return could once more lead to internal struggles and infighting. Thus, the Russian authorities decided to keep Karađorđe and his associates in Russia under close surveillance. Karađorđe was stationed in the town of Novomyrhorod (Новомиргород), in modern-day Ukraine, which was at the time one of the centers of Serbian immigrants to Russia, and the capital of *New Serbia* between 1752 and 1764. There, Karađorđe came into contact with the members of a Greek secret society, known as the *Filiki Eteria*. This secret organization had for its goal the liberation of all Christian peoples under the rule of the Ottoman Empire, and the forming of a Christian federation in the Balkans. Karađorđe became a member of this society and vowed to work towards the liberation of oppressed Christians. The members of Filiki Eteria saw him as a valuable addition to their ranks, as he was a respected and seasoned freedom fighter. With their assistance, Karađorđe was given false papers with which he managed to cross unopposed into Serbia, once more returning to his homeland.

His return came as a huge surprise. At once he went to his own groom, Vujica Vulićević, as one of the men he thought he could trust. However, unbeknownst to him, Vulićević was now fully a paid man of Miloš Obrenović. The latter was immediately informed, and he promptly ordered the death of Karađorđe. Vujica Vulićević thus ordered one of his aides to murder Karađorđe. The hero of the First Serbian Uprising was thus murdered with an axe while sleeping in his tent in oak grove of Radovanje, on July 13th, 1817. His body was beheaded, and his head sent to Marashli Ali Pasha in Belgrade. The latter had the head flayed, stuffed, and sent to the Sultan himself in Constantinople. There it was displayed at the gates, impaled on a spike for seven days. Such a vile death of the storied and elevated Serbian hero was certainly uncalled for but at the time seen as the only logical termination of the threat that Karađorđe brought. His martyr's death gained Miloš Obrenović even less popularity amongst the people, and his opposition grew even stronger. The memory of Karađorđe, and all of his glorious deeds however, still lived on in the people, and would never be forgotten. Moreover, in the decades that followed these events, the descendants of the two men - the Obrenović and Karađorđević families would continuously feud over the Serbian throne. This feud would end in 1903 with the assassination of Alexander Obrenović, and the ascension of Petar Karađorđević to the throne. Today, the Royal Dynasty of Serbia is the Karađorđević dynasty.

After these events, the fighting of the Serbian Revolution was effectively over. Both the First and the Second Serbian Uprising were the instrumental catalysts that ushered the fate of Serbia in a new direction. Through the crucible of fire towards clearer skies - the Serbian nation had to suffer to overcome its difficult position. And it is at this point that our story can end: many historians end the story of the Serbian Revolution at year 1817. However, there are those that incorporate the later developments into it as well, the diplomatic struggles that led to the eventual recognition of the Serbian state, extending the period of the Serbian Revolution to 1833. We shall talk of this last stage as well.

Now, even though the armed conflicts were finished, and the Serbs received some amount of semi-independence, the struggle was not fully over. There were a lot of factors that did not work in the favor of the Ottomans, and that is why they were exceptionally lenient towards Miloš Obrenović. Firstly, they wanted to avoid Russian mediation and involvement (chiefly due to the unfulfilled Treaty of Bucharest) which was becoming a great possibility. The Ottoman government did not want to give the Serbs the proposed self-government in the exact way that they wanted it. Thus they advised the Marashli Ali Pasha to be lenient, forgiving, and to not spare his promises, in order to calm the Serbs and keep the Russians at bay.

Secondly, the situation within Constantinople was far from ideal. The unrest and the revolts in the Ottoman Empire did not stop with the overthrow of Sultan Selim III and the cancelling of his questionable reforms. Tensions were at an all-time high within the Ottoman Empire. Particularly dangerous were the increasingly insurrectionist movements of unhappy Muslims in Bosnia, which had begun during the reign of Selim III, and which could not be completely stifled. After the infamous Suleyman Pasha Skopljak, the Vizier of Bosnia, did not manage to silence the rebellious voices there, he was replaced in 1818. A string of viziers exchanged places in the following years, without success.

Furious, the Ottoman sultan then sent Ali Jalaluddin Pasha, who was known for his determination and ruthlessness, to bring order into Bosnia. Jalaluddin came to his new position in the early spring of 1820 and immediately began a string of harsh measures. He had to conquer the renegade cities of Mostar and Srebrenica. This crisis in Bosnia was just one of the several hardships that befell the frail and ailing Ottoman Empire in these decisive years. That is why the Ottomans could not risk instigating any new revolts within Serbia, and thus were lenient with them.

The critical turning point in the entire situation was brought about by the death of Tsar Alexander on November 19th, 1825. Only then, in the anticipation of a new and uncertain course of the Russian politics, did the Ottoman government release one half of the members of the Serbian deputation that were held in Constantinople as envoys, but kept the other half in Constantinople in the patriarchate - under supervision. After the death of Alexander, the zealous and energetic Tsar Nicholas I came to the Russian throne. He quickly settled on decisive steps, which his late brother was thinking about before the end of his rule. As early as March of 1826, the Russian government sent an ultimatum to the Ottomans in Constantinople, requesting that they fulfill their demands. Amongst these demands was the issue of the Serbian self-government. The Ottomans agreed to negotiate. However, in 1826 Constantinople was shaken by yet another insurrection, this time amongst its own core. In May of that year, the Sultan completely ended the order of the *janissaries*, much to their dismay. A small unrest was immediately quelled, but this left the Ottoman army immensely weakened and in dire need of reforms. All of this didn't leave them much choice but to enter into the negotiations with the Russians and to accept almost everything that was wanted from them.

This led to the first such treaty, the Akkerman Convention. Signed on October 7th 1826, amongst other things the convention also tackled the Serbian question: in article 5 of this treaty, autonomy for the Principality of Serbia was given, as well as the return of lands removed in 1813. The Serbs were also granted freedom of movement throughout the Ottoman Empire.

However, soon after the Russo-Turkish war of 1828-1829 erupted, resulting from - amongst other factors - from the Sultan Mahmud II's rejection of the Akkerman Treaty. However - as could be expected - the Ottomans catastrophically lost in this war to the Russians. The result was the Treaty of Adrianople, signed on September 14th, 1829 in the city of Adrianople. Under this treaty several important decisions were made, but for our story, the most important one was the formal Ottoman guarantee of Serbian autonomy. Thus, the Peace of Adrianople is one of the most important moments in the entire Serbian history of the 19th century.

This treaty truly secured the much coveted autonomy for Serbia and secured its international position. Of course, one can clearly understand the sheer enormity of the role that Russia played here. In the end it came through as a staunch ally and fought to decisively bring about the autonomy that many gave their lives for. In a way, it also established the real and legal continuity between the First and Second Serbian Uprisings; i.e. between what Karađorđe began and what Miloš Obrenović finished. On September 18, the Sultan issued an act on self-government, which was officially registered in Belgrade on December 2 and which was announced to the National Assembly in Kragujevac. All of these guarantees were later formalized and legalized with the so-called Hatt-i-Shariff (official Ottoman document) of 1830, which was ceremoniously declared in Belgrade on the day of Saint Andrew the Apostle. Simultaneously, Miloš Obrenović was legally recognized as the hereditary prince of the Serbian state, which was the official beginning of his royal dynasty. With all of these acts, Serbia at last became a European state, with its own dynasty, and under the Ottoman sovereignty and Russian protection. It was also symbolic, many centuries after the end of the Medieval Serbian state, a new one was resurrected on the same spot.

The Serbian Forces in the Revolution period and Their Fight

THERE WERE MANY FACTORS that dictated the nature of the warfare in the Serbian Revolution. If we compare it to the concurrent wars and battles that marked the Napoleonic Era, it quickly becomes clear that the Serbian Revolution was in numerous ways severely archaic. The main reason for this was the overall influence of the Ottoman Empire. Already ailing and frail during the Napoleonic Era - and especially afterwards - the Ottoman Empire was severely outdated in many aspects. Culturally, it was highly traditional and conservative, limited to an extreme extent by the confines of their religion. Militarily too, the Ottomans were far behind their contemporaries, the Russians, Austrians, and the French. Western Europe made numerous breakthroughs and innovations in warfare, modernizing it to a great extent - however these were slow to travel to the Balkans. The Serbs, being a subject of the Ottoman Empire at the time, were in great measure influenced by the Empire they were a part of - which can only be considered natural after several centuries of Ottoman occupation. Thus it was that when the First Serbian Uprising erupted, the Serbs were in many ways constrained in their warfare, due to the fact that they were in most parts as outdated as their overlords. However, with each year of the Serbian Revolution that passed, the foreign influences on the conflict grew and the Serbian Revolution quickly gained a unique character, making it stand out distinctly in the entire Napoleonic Era.

Here it is important to remember that the Serbian people lived not only as subjects of the Ottoman Empire, but also the other neighboring Empires. Just across the river from Belgrade was then Austrian territory, and the Serbs dwelt there as well. On the other side, across the River Drina, the Serbs lived in the region of Bosnia and beyond of modern day Croatia. In this latter region was the famed Austrian Military Frontier, of which the Serb frontiersmen were an integral part. Thus, it is important to mention that these Serbs from Austria, and those Serbs living under Ottoman occupation, had entirely different standards. Austria at the time was a modern empire, with many more freedoms and opportunities. The Austrian Military Frontier thus gave rise to many prominent, learned Serbs, who rose to lofty positions culturally and militarily in Austrian service. These Serbs would also come to play an important part in the Serbian Revolution, many of them fleeing to their heartland in order to support their freedom-fighting brethren. Their valuable experiences in Russian and Austrian military service would come to be a big aspect for Serbian successes in the conflict. Karađorđe himself served with the Austrians before the Uprising and his veterancy gave him a significant upper hand over some of the less skilled Ottoman commanders. Moreover, in the later stages of the uprising, with the arrival of the Russian agents and then the Russian military aid, standards went up even further, and many modern changes were brought to the Serbian freedom fighters.

When observing the historic depictions and literary sources in relation to the Serbian Revolution, most casual readers will be quick to determine that there wasn't a lot of visual difference between the standard Ottoman or Serb forces. In some aspects there is truth to this, but not entirely. One of the major similarities between these two armies was their dress. In the earliest stages of the uprising, the Serbs were officially declared insurgents, and as such did not possess a standardized uniform pattern. Most fighters were volunteers and conscripts, and fought in regional, folk dress. However, over the centuries of Ottoman rule, this dress acquired numerous Oriental influences. Thus it was that the high ranking Serb leaders - the voivodes and the knyazes - wore a mainly Ottoman-styled outfit. Nevertheless, similarities ended here for the most part. The outfit of a common Serb fighter still displayed a variety of traditional Slavic elements, and that made for fairly easy distinguishing. The Ottomans preferred *turban* hats, *şalvar* trousers, *kaftan* long robes, and usually brightly colored and richly decorated clothes. A common Serbian peasant on the other hand, wore roughspun undyed fabrics, traditional Slavic embroidered wool, and the unmistakable traditional Serb footwear - the leather *opanci* shoes. Another great aspect of their differences was hair-related. The Serbs at the time of the First Uprising still adhered to their millenia old Slavic tradition of wearing a long braid at the back of the head. Men shaved the frontal part of the head, but left the rear covered with hair, which was grown long and braided. This tradition can be observed amongst almost all Slavic peoples and cultures, and has very old roots. The Turks however, shaved their heads clean as was their custom, and this made for a clear difference.

In the later stages of the uprising Karađorđe explicitly ordered that the soldiers were to cut off their traditional braids - most likely for tactical reasons, for convenience in battle. One popular tale states that the Ottomans could easily parade the decapitated heads of Serbian fighters by holding them by this braid, so Karađorđe sought to put an end to that tradition. A more probable reason is simply a following of European trends. Nevertheless, the order was never fully put to action, as the Serbian men were hard to part from their long braids which were seen as a major symbol of manhood.

Even in the early stages of the uprising, the Serbs made certain attempts at standardizing their wear and having at least a semblance of standard uniforms. Karađorđe, relying on his experience in the Austrian Freikorps, understood the importance of a regular and well outfitted army. Even then he understood that a successful army depended on good training and all the regularities, especially when fighting against an enemy such as the Ottomans, who often lacked cohesion and complex tactics. Very early on, Karađorđe assembled a battalion of so-called "regular men", to act as a form of a standing army. These regulars were assembled from both experienced and young fighters from all over the region. Several sources point out that these regular soldiers were stationed in the barracks of the Belgrade fortress, and that they were given Russian uniforms - or uniforms derived from those. Thus we can observe that at least a part of the Serbian fighting force in the Revolution was dressed almost the same as some of the regular Russian troops of the Napoleonic wars. It is further claimed that these uniforms were worn by officers, cannoneers, and drummers of the common formations of the uprising, while the other, common recruits wore a mix of folk clothes and uniform elements. These uniform elements were most commonly carrying pouches for cartridges, gunpowder, and projectiles, and similar accoutrements.

When weapons are considered, it is important to note that there was a great variety of what was on offer. In the later stages of the uprising, most of the regular soldiers carried muskets with added bayonets, with accompanying cold weapons. Officers and voivodes on the other hand, often relied on traditional weaponry of the time - pistols, swords, sabres, and yataghan daggers.

In many ways it is agreed by historians that Karađorđe managed to create and train a small-sized standing army in roughly 3 months, and worked to make it into a reliable fighting force that could easily stand shoulder to shoulder with other modern European units of the time.

Cavalry too was given special attention as the uprising evolved. It was undoubtedly greatly inspired by the Russian Cossack regiments that entered Serbia under the commands of Joseph Cornelius O'Rourke and Ivan Ivanovich Isaev and went on to score great victories against the Ottomans. Throughout history the Serbs boasted highly skilled mounted troops, and were exceptionally prized in foreign service. Serbian Hussars were highly influential on the development of cavalry units in European military history. In the decades preceding the First Serbian Uprising, a good amount of influential Serbs emigrated to Russia at the instigation of the Russian Empress. In the territories created there - New Serbia and Slavoserbia - these Serb settlers formed distinguished cavalry units that served in the Russian Empire. Most notably these were the *Bakhmut Hussar Regiment* formed in 1764, and the *Serbian Hussar Regiment*, formed in 1724. These units fought with distinction in the Seven Years' War, Russo-Swedish War, and the War of the Polish Succession.

When the Russian troops entered Serbia in the First Uprising, there were reports that amongst this force was a Serbian Cossack Regiment, organized by one Colonel Nikić, and utilizing Wallachian Pandur troops. However, when the Russians left Serbia in 1812, the French consul reported that they left behind one cossack regiment composed entirely of Serbs. This French consul also reports that by 1813, the Serbian Cossack Corps was established, and wore uniforms of the Russian cossacks.

Artillery also played a crucial role in the Serbian Revolution. Undoubtedly less established as in the European armies, the artillery was the most fearsome weapon in the Balkan conflicts. It held a great fear factor, as it was a devastating field weapon. However, both the Ottomans and the Serbs lacked them in sufficient numbers. In the opening stages of the uprising, the Serbs had virtually no cannons, and had to rely on plunder and gains from their victories in order to establish a meager artillery core. An interesting insight into the fear factor an artillery piece had in the Balkans is the anecdote from the first days of the Uprising, when Karađorđe ordered a skilled craftsman to create two cannons made from cherry tree logs. These were made with high precision and banded with steel rings for strength. However, their battlefield potential was next to none: they were inaccurate, had a short range, and were dangerous to handle and unsafe. But Karađorđe most likely had them made to raise the morale of his troops - many of them considered this a major and advanced weapon. The cherry-tree cannons *were* used in the initial battles of the uprising, but mostly as a signal weapon.

However, with what was gained from their victories, and what was given to them by their allies, the Serbs soon fielded a good amount of cannons, and artillery was a critical component in each battle. After 1806, the initial Russian military supplies started arriving into Serbian hands. While these were mostly rifles, some cannons found their way as well. Field Marshal Michelson advised General Isaev - as the Russians were relocating to Wallachia - that he was to take 6 cannons from his own complements, and transfer them to the Serbs. Thus it is reported that Karađorđe received 4 six-pound and 2 three-pound calibre cannons from the Odessa Artillery Garrison, with all the necessary supplies and ammunition. This was undoubtedly a great boon for his forces. Almost a year later, on August 11th 1808, another 6 cannons with all the necessities and ammo carts were sent to the Serbs from Jassy in Moldova. More cannons were sent in July of 1809 by Count Prozorovsky: 2 bronze cannons with complete ammunition complements, and one thousand rifles as well. A similar shipment followed in the next year, and the year after that. By June 1811, on the order of Kutuzov himself, a shipment of 10 cannons and 10 cases of ammunition were sent to Serbia. This was the last such shipment that is recorded.

Furthermore, it is worth mentioning that the Serbs were quick to establish their own cannon foundry in Belgrade, which began operating as early as 1807. The foundry was located in Belgrade, and early on cannon balls were produced in it successfully. Then, in 1808, the first cannon was made in it, and following this, Russian master foundrymen were sent to Serbia, and a quite acceptable rate of cannons were produced. These Russian experts were K. Kalinin and one Polyakov. Thus it was that, step by step, one cannon after the other, the

Serbian artillery grew larger and larger, and gave them a considerable fighting chance. Undoubtedly, the Serbian cannon foundry, the aid from the Russians, as well as the cannons they captured in battle, were all a great boost for Serbian military capabilities in the Uprising, and certainly lifted their morale as well.

Another very interesting aspect of the use of artillery in the Serbian Revolution is undoubtedly the use of rockets. Rocket artillery found its place in the Napoleonic Wars: Congreve rockets were developed in Britain in 1804, and quickly found its use in the war in Europe. Military history records that this rocket artillery was first used efficiently in the Raid on Boulogne in 1804 against the French. However, funnily enough, such rockets found their way to distant Serbia. Around early 1806, the chief Serbian representative, Mateja Nenadović, stayed in Vienna, and it is reported that from here he brought back "*1,000 pieces of large rockets*", made in Saxony. Without a doubt this weapon was seen as a major novelty in the Serbian uprising. It is reported that these rockets were promptly utilized with considerable success: they were used to utterly decimate the Ottoman defences at Šabac. Two years later, a Serbian trader from Austria, one Marko Dobrić, made attempts to smuggle an official British manufacturing plan for these rockets, but was intercepted and the plans confiscated by the Austrians. This allowed them to create a prototype series of 24 rocket artillery pieces, in the workshops of Oberfeuerwerkmeister Mager. By 1814, the Austrians boasted their first rocket equipped unit. A bit earlier, around 1812, the Serbs also managed to create a somewhat more primitive version of these rockets, undoubtedly wishing to repeat its devastating effects on the enemy army. One surviving note by Karađorđe implies this: "*It was written to the Council that the artillery officer is granted all that he needs for the manufacturing of rockets.*" The Serbian rockets utilized a specially crafted frame, and a cannon ball as the projectile. The whole weapon weighed no more than 10 kilograms, and the propellant was fired by ordinary fuses. Reports indicate that the range greatly varied - from 800 to 2,000 meters. However, they were quite inaccurate, and didn't catch on.

Another great feature of the Serbian strategy in the revolution was the use of complex earthworks, palisades, and improvised fortifications. The nature of the uprising, and the fact that the Serbs were often outnumbered and on the defence, led to them naturally adapting to the situations on the battlefield, and relying on solid defensive points to gain an upper hand over their enemies. Their use of trenches and palisades was reported very early on in the uprising, and from that point on it became an almost constant feature of every battle. However, with each year and battle that passed, these fortifications became more complex and much more effective. They evolved from primitive trenches to much more advanced redoubts and flèches, and then to very well made palisades and similar features. When done ideally, these entrenchments allowed the Serbian soldiers to lay down effective and accurate fire on the enemy while exposing as little of their body as possible. Without a doubt that this strategy had a great effect on the survivability rate of the common Serbian soldier, and certainly gave them a much needed upper hand. Field fortifications that they made were always well camouflaged, and enhanced with further field work: dug in gunpowder magazines, crew quarters, and so on.

When redoubts and fortifications were not a possibility or were limited, the Serbs utilized modern European battlefield tactics that again gave them a fighting chance. The "care" formation is one of these, known popularly as the infantry square formation - one of the defining aspects of Napoleonic Era warfare. The square formation was a great form of defence against cavalry charges, and also gave an enhanced rate of fire. Karađorđe and many of his commanders learned of these tactics while serving with the Austrians and the Russians in the years preceding the uprising. Their veterancy clearly paid off here: in the majority of the battles led in the First Serbian Uprising, the Serbs were clearly superior in their tactics on the battlefield, as well as their mastery of the developing situation of a battle. This is also clearly proved in the amount of victories that they had.

Conclusion
The Wolven Creed

THE STORY OF THE SERBIAN Revolution - no matter how difficult or hard to grasp - is not the only such story in the Balkans. The flames that spread even before the onset of the Napoleonic Wars quickly spread towards the east, and engulfed the fragile state of affairs in the Balkans. The Ottoman Empire at the time was the "museum piece of Europe", an odd vestige of a bygone era. In many ways, its fate was already sealed and it was destined to crumble in the wake of new and revolutionary tides that swept through Europe. Many other nations and ethnicities that suffered under its oppressive rule were bolstered and encouraged to fight for independence not only by the French Revolution, but also by the Serbian revolution, which was the first to erupt in the Balkans. The Serbian Revolution marked the very beginning of an era of national awakenings in the Balkans, which were the crucial component of the unfolding Eastern Question.

Nevertheless, the story of these uprisings is as sorrowful as much as it is inspirational. The Serbian people suffered greatly in their history: from their earliest struggles against the Byzantines, through their fight for independence in the middle ages, all the way to the rapid decline in the face of unstoppable Ottoman invasions - their struggle was almost constant. But it is said that hard times breed hard people: in the case of Serbia this is most certainly true. A nation fragmented by several empires, it never lost its burning desire for freedom and independence. The oppressed peoples became revolutionaries, freedom fighters, brigands, and guerilla warriors. And throughout these centuries, they showed to the conquerors that one cannot place shackles on wolves and eagles - they will fight ever harder and soar ever higher, to those lofty heights where freedom is eternal.

By Aleksa Vučković

References:

Bataković, D. 2006. *A Balkan-Style French Revolution? The 1804 Serbian Uprising in European Perspective*. Balcanica.

Meriage, L. 1978. *The First Serbian Uprising (1804-1813) and the Nineteenth-Century Origins of the Eastern Question*. Slavic Review.

Sowage, S. 2009. *The Serbian Revolution and the Serbian State*. Twenty-Five Lectures on Modern Balkan History.

Various. 2007. *Тицанова Буна 1807*. MZ Voganj.

Богдановић, Б. *Артиљерија у Првом Српском Устанку*.

Јаковљевић, J. *Српско-турски преговори о миру 1808*. Пројекат Растко.

Поповић, В. *Европа и Српско Питање у Периоду Ослобођења 1804-1918*. Catena Mundi.

Ћоровић, В. *Историја Срба*.

Златковић, Б. 2007. *Први Српски Устанак у Говору и у Твору*. Институт за Књижевност и Уметност Београд.

Understanding Less Familiar Terms:

1. *Knyaz; knez; кнез* - A historical Slavic title, used to denote a Duke or a Prince.

2. *Voivode; voyvode; војвода* - A historical Slavic title, denoting a war leader, a warlord; here an a respected leader of men.

3. *Pasha; Paşa* - An Ottoman Turkish honorary title and rank, denoting a governor, general, dignitary, or any other respected official.

4. *Syrmia; Srem* - A fertile historical region northwest of Belgrade, now in modern day Serbia. During the period covered in this book it was a part of Austria.

5. *Military Frontier* - the borderland region of Austria that acted as the buffer zone to stop Ottoman incursions. It was populated mostly by Slavs: Serbs and Croats, and other Christian ethnicities.

6. *Tsar* - a royal title used amongst the Slavic nations; derived from Latin *caesar* and denotes an Emperor.

7. *Vizier; Grand Vizier* - a high ranking political advisor or minister in the Ottoman Empire.

8. *Dahije; Dahijas* - renegade *janissary* officers who took power in the Pashalik of Belgrade and took up tyrannical rule.

9. *Pashalik* - denotes a territory administered by and under the jurisdiction of a *pasha* (see above).

10. *Janissary* - Elite Ottoman infantry units that occupied important and high positions.

11. *Palisade* - a defensive wall or perimeter usually made from sharpened wooden stakes.

12. *Redoubt* - a defensive perimeter of enclosed emplacement usually made of earthworks.

13. *Flèche* - a defensive, arrow shaped perimeter and a part of a fortification system.

Don't miss out!

Visit the website below and you can sign up to receive emails whenever History Nerds publishes a new book. There's no charge and no obligation.

https://books2read.com/r/B-A-ODOK-JEVLB

Connecting independent readers to independent writers.

Also by History Nerds

Celtic History
Ireland

Great Wars of the World
World War 1
World War 2
The Napoleonic Wars: One Shot at Glory
The Serbian Revolution: 1804-1835
Peace Won by the Saber: The Crimean War, 1853-1856
The Wars of the Roses

Irish Heroes
Grace O'Malley: The Pirate Queen of Ireland
William Butler Yeats: Nobel Prize Winning Poet
Scáthach
Finn McCool

The History of the Vikings

Vikings
Longships on Restless Seas

The Rise and Fall of Empires
Rome: The Rise and Fall

Standalone
The History of the United Kingdom
The History of Ireland
The History of America
Stalin
The Fiery Maelstrom of Freedom
The History of Scotland
Robert the Bruce
William Wallace: Scotland's Great Freedom Fighter
The History of Wales